The Path After Grace

The Path After Grace

The Journey

Nicki Corinne White

Carpenter's Son Publishing

Path after Grace

Published by Carpenter's Son Publishing, Franklin, Tennessee

Cover Design and Interior Design by Suzanne Lawing

Front Cover - Photo by Nicki White

Printed in the United States of America

ISBN: 978-1-968127-06-0 (print)

DEDICATION

To my children: Jessica, Emily, Nathan and Brianna Mae

I was thinking about ways I have grown through the years, and even though God is still working on me and has me on a journey of maturing in Christ, I know that being a mom has made me more committed to God. On days I wanted to give up, I couldn't, because I want you all to love God and grow in Him. I could never quit learning and growing.

My heart loves you so very much, and I want you in eternity with God, and to be serving Him here on our brief time on earth. I praise God for each of you, and I will never stop praying for your own journeys.

Contents

"If you can trust God to save you for eternity, you can trust Him to lead you for a lifetime."

- David Platt

Introduction

"But we should always give thanks to God for you, brethren beloved by the Lord, because God has chosen you from the beginning for salvation through sanctification by the Spirit and faith in the truth."
2 THESSALONIANS 2:13

Do you fully trust God?

I do, yet at the same time I'm also an over thinker, and I have spent far too much time in my life overthinking everything, including how to mature in my faith. I lament sin, which I should. I do not always feel victorious, which isn't good. I pray to be more effective in my study of God's Word, and pray for God to guide me in my walk. I am sure there are many reasons and aspects of what causes growth in our Christian faith. It is not really something we think about. It is something we do. We listen to God's Word being taught, we pray, we read our Bibles, and we have friends share their faith with us.

So many factors draw us closer to God. And some hinder us.

These things will all be addressed in this book, but most importantly we'll delve into what God says from His Word.

The biblical definition of sanctification is *the process of being set apart for God's use, or made holy, transforming someone to be more like*

Jesus. We don't instantly become the perfect Christian, always doing what is right. It is a journey. A process. It is a lifelong path we are on. Sometimes we take wrong turns, and sometimes it takes forever to learn a lesson, BUT He loves us and has drawn us to Himself for His purposes.

> *"Therefore, putting aside all malice and all deceit and hypocrisy and envy and all slander, and like newborn babies, long for the pure milk of the word, so that by it you may grow in respect to salvation, if you have tasted the kindness of the Lord." 1 Peter 2:1-2*

The word "therefore" connects the previous section describing a believer's identity in Christ. The next section tells us to get rid of all malice and bitterness from our life. It continues and tells us to eliminate deceit and hypocrisy, envy and speaking falsely. Then we can begin to grow in our faith, and experience the restoration that God gives us in Jesus Christ His Son. This may take time, but it means that through time, we should expect to make slow progress toward the goal of becoming more like Christ: loving, humble, kind, self-controlled. Working to rid oneself of sin is how we can make room for God to work in our lives.

I was recently reading my copy of "Streams In The Desert," a book that every human should read! If you don't have a copy of this book, I highly recommend getting one.

The author writes;

> *"Therefore I am well content with weaknesses, with insults, with distresses, with persecutions, with difficulties, for Christ's sake; for when I am weak, then I am strong. 2 Corinthians 12:10 (KJV)*

What really caught my attention was what she says about this passage. *"Here is the secret of divine all-sufficiency, to come to an end of everything in ourselves and in our circumstances. When we reach this place, we will stop asking for sympathy because of our hard situation or bad treatment, for we will recognize these things as the very conditions of our blessing and we will turn from them to God and find them a claim upon Him."*[1] In essence, she is urging us to reconsider our focus on our circumstances and accept it as part of God's divine plan. Isn't that a beautiful perspective to have? How many times have you, or I, analyzed our current problems and prayed for God to remove the very thing that would later lead to growth? We cannot see the big picture. But there is no doubt that we must trust Him, in order to finish strong.

The author, Mrs. Charles E. Coleman, continues by quoting George Matheson, the well known blind preacher from Scotland. *"My God I have not thanked thee for my thorn. I have thanked thee a thousand times for my roses, but not once for my thorn. ...teach me the value of my thorn."*[2] What an incredibly powerful plea!

This is so me. Is it you too? I try to look for the good but never truly get past the pain. I can see how God has used something for His good but often forget that it is a continual process.

What is it that I need to embrace to understand His plan? It begins with God's grace, and acknowledging that I need Him. That is the answer to my questioning heart. I am lost without Him. He grants me grace, and directs me through this journey of life.

Looking up the word "grace" one gets many definitions. Our biblical answer stems from grace being the center of what we believe. We believe we are saved by faith through grace. We usually define it as unmerited favor. Undeserved. We count on it to rescue us from a fiery eternity. Scripture is filled with so many verses about grace. So many

---

1 Mrs. Charles E. Cowman, *Streams in the Desert,* (Grand Rapids, MI: Zondervan Publishing House, 1996), 114-115.

2 Mrs. Charles E. Cowman, *Streams in the Desert,* (Grand Rapids, MI: Zondervan Publishing House, 1996), 114-115.

in fact, that I think sometimes it is often just a rote word thrown into conversation. That should not be the case.

> *"And God is able to make all grace abound to you, so that always having all sufficiency in everything, you may have an abundance for every good deed." 2 Corinthians 9:8*

I love the phrase "having all sufficiency in everything" - God gives us everything we need. That says it all, doesn't it? Perhaps if we fully trusted God we would not lean on our own understanding ever again.

I did not grow up in a Christian home when I was young. When my adopted dad died I was only 13. My mom, sister and I became Christians through a series of events after his death. Times were so hard, and I knew I had God to walk through those times with me, but for decades I struggled to feel like I was worthy of God's love. Like **many** decades.

How could an almighty God, who is creator of all things, all-knowing, righteous and powerful, love me with all my flaws? I knew He wanted me to walk in obedience and serve Him, so I continued reading my Bible, worked in various ministries, and hoped that someday I would become a mature Christian. After years went by and I still felt I was not on the path God wanted me on, I finally understood that attaining maturity in Christ is a lifelong process. It is also not just "doing" things, but a heart attitude. I needed to continue to put one foot in front of the other to be truly set apart and transformed. I met other believers also struggling with this, and I tried to encourage them to remain in the Word, spend time with other Christians, and listen to Godly teachers. Then they would continue to grow. It is not a quick thing. At funerals you often hear, "they kept the faith."

Do not give up, dear one. Keep the faith. God gives us everything we need!

In Dane Ortland's book, "Gentle and Lowly," I appreciate this thought from the very first page… It fits with this book. "*This book is written for the discouraged, the frustrated, the weary, the disenchanted, the cynical, the empty. Those running on fumes. Those whose Christian lives feel like constantly running up a descending escalator. Those of us who find ourselves thinking; 'How could I mess up that bad--again?' It is for that increasing suspicion that God's patience with us is wearing thin. For those of us who know God loves us but suspect we have deeply disappointed Him. We have told others of the love of Christ yet wonder if--as for us--he harbors mild resentment. Who wonder if we have shipwrecked our lives beyond what can be repaired. Who are convinced we've permanently diminished our usefulness to the Lord.*"[3]

Do you feel this way? Maybe not all the time, but sometimes? We can unconsciously allow these types of thoughts to sneak in, and when we are weak, they can take over causing us to be disheartened. But I am certain that feelings of anxiety and defeat are not what God has in mind for us, and because of that I will strive to ignore them. I do not want to lose heart, and I do not want you to, either.

For the past several years, my goal in ministry has been to do as much as I can to share the gospel with those who need to hear it. I also have wanted to encourage others in their walk of faith, and show them ways they could share God's grace with others. Even when I was struggling with my own life, I always wanted to share my faith.

Paul tells Philemon,

> *"... I hear of your love and of the faith which you have toward the Lord Jesus and toward all the saints; and I pray that the fellowship of your faith may become effective through the knowledge of every good thing which is in you for Christ's sake. Philemon 1:5-6*

---

3 Dane Ortlund, *Gentle and Lowly,* (Wheaton, IL: Crossway, 2020), 13.

Philemon had been saved under Paul's ministry, probably in Ephesus. Philemon was wealthy and had a large household. He had a slave named Onesimus. Onesimus was not a believer at the time, and stole money from Philemon, then ran away. He fled to Rome and met Paul, and cared for him while Paul was in prison. Onesimus becomes a believer, and Paul later asks Philemon to forgive his slave Onesimus, and take him back. This letter to Philemon was sent with Onesimus. The above verses are showing us, as believers, to love others, especially others in the household of faith. Paul was sending a message to the church that as believers, we belong to each other in our faith. Other believers in our life are an integral part of our walk. God can use them to point us to Him.

I read someone's message about our sanctification process, and it was mentioned that as we grow we become more steady in our faith. This is very true; it is a journey, a path that takes us up and down, up hills and over ravines, through the forest and rough waters. James tells us in James 1:2-8,

> *"Consider it all joy , my brethren, when you encounter various trials, knowing that the testing of your faith produces endurance. And let endurance have its perfect result, so that you may be perfect and complete, lacking in nothing. But if any of you lacks wisdom, let him ask of God, who gives to all generously and without reproach, and it will be given to him. But he must ask in faith without any doubting, for the one who doubts is like the surf of the sea, driven and tossed by the wind. For that man ought not to expect that he will receive anything from the Lord, being a double minded man, unstable in all his ways."*

I had a friend tell me that we should all be stable, not wavering. While this may be true, I did not have the experiences early in life they did, surrounded by positive Christians encouraging me in my faith. It took a while for me to learn. Growing up, I did not learn about Daniel, David, Ruth and all the other people in the Bible.

How then do we become stable? How does it happen? Is it quick or does it take time?

I contemplated several topics for this book project, but knew I needed to address this; not just for myself but for all those reading this who follow Christ.

And so this book was born. I hope you enjoy the ride. Let us study the fullness of grace and how we have life abundant as we follow His path. I believe with my whole heart that He loves you and wants you to have fullness of joy. He is a merciful, loving God and is waiting for you to see Him clearly as you mature in your faith.

"I have held many things in my hands, and I have lost them all; but whatever I have placed in God's hands, that I still possess."

- Martin Luther

CHAPTER ONE

For His Own Purpose

"Who has saved us and called us with a holy calling, not according to our works, but according to His own purpose and grace which was granted us in Christ Jesus from all eternity."

2 TIMOTHY 1:9

I was sitting in my Junior High School science class, circa 1972, and heard a siren. My friend next to me was trying to guess what kind. Was it a police car or fire engine? I did not know until later that it was, in fact, headed to my home. It was around noon, I think. Later that afternoon I got off the bus with my sister, Lisa, and we were puzzled at the fact that our Grandpa was the one picking us up. You see we had a very long driveway, and many times our dad would pick us up from the bus stop. We looked at each other and thought something might be wrong. Our first inclination was that something had happened to Grandma, but then Grandpa would be with her, and not picking us up. We were confused.

As we approached the house, we saw our moma run inside.

We got out of the car and bolted inside behind her, trying to comprehend what was going on.

She turned to us and said, “Your father has died.”

Lisa ran to her room. I stood there shocked for a moment, and then I ran to mine. Yes, we left her standing there all alone, which had its own ramifications.

We were all now alone yet together, isolating in grief. It was the way we would be now as a smaller family. So many questions enveloped each one of us that night as we replayed his last moments in our imagination.

What had happened? What would we do? A feeling of dread enveloped me. We were told he had a heart attack, fell off the tractor, and could not be revived.

We had 31 horses, and we were out of hay in our barn. Dad had been going to a nearby farm to get more when he had the heart attack. SO many things had to immediately be taken care of. That very day.

Within the month we had to sell 28 horses, and life changed forever once again. I cried my eyes out as I watched trucks drive them away down our long driveway. What was to become of us? We had no income.

Moma, as we had always called her, was 56 and had not worked in years outside the farm. We had not been attending any church, and the funeral director suggested we contact a young pastor whose father had died when he was young; (he often did funerals) so we had him officiate our dad’s.

As a teen, I thought he was old, but he may have been about 30. Thinking back on this, and now knowing him for 40+ years, he was probably greatly concerned for us, even burdened, and I know he prayed for us. A couple of months later, he came down to the farm and invited us to his little Baptist church. The three of us went, and I was amazed. Everyone had a Bible! They were memorizing Romans 12:1-2 as a congregation.

Therefore I urge you, brethren, by the mercies of God, to present your bodies a living and holy sacrifice, acceptable to God, which is your spiritual service of worship. And do not be conformed to this world, but be transformed by the renewing of your mind, so that you may prove what the will of God is, that which is good and acceptable and perfect.

I had never heard of it before. As a matter of fact, I didn't even know people memorized Scripture. Everyone visited, and showed each other how much they cared for each other. We went to youth group that night, and ended up attending that little church every week. Within a few months my moma, sister and I accepted Christ's free gift of salvation, and a new journey began.

I did not understand everything about God or how He had actually called us to Him at the time, but this was the step I took. Not without hard times, BUT we now had hope in Christ.

If you've ever experienced a traumatic moment like the loss of a loved one, you know how powerful the presence of God is, during your time of grief. Everything about Him is enhanced, tangible, and supernaturally real. It is in our darkest hour, when we need Him the most.

I did not fully understand all things Christian at the time, but one thing I knew as a young believer: I must study His Word. And then maybe, just maybe I could become who He wanted me to be. In J.I. Packer's book, "A Quest For Godliness" he says, "*The healthy Christian is not necessarily the extrovert, ebullient Christian, but the Christian who has a sense of God's presence stamped deep on his soul, who trembles at God's Word, who lets it dwell in him richly by constant meditation upon it, and who tests and reforms his life daily in response to it.*"[4] I believe, like Packer, that we must let our study of God's Word

4 J.I. Packer, *A Quest for Godliness* (Wheaton, IL: Crossway Books, 1990), 116.

be a priority in our life. My desire is to know God so thoroughly that I tremble at God's Word, and that I seek His face in all I do.

Some people get saved and instantly start reading their Bible. I did read it as a new believer but only parts. Not straight through. One thing I have learned from mentoring young women is that many newer believers study the New Testament over and over. Which is good, but the Old Testament tells us who God is, that He is holy and just, full of mercy and truth. It is essential for us to grasp these concepts and study all of God's Word and not just part of it.

Someone told me a few years later that without becoming a believer in Christ one cannot fully understand scripture. I have always remembered that. I cannot expect unbelievers to understand God's Word, but one must take that first step of believing in Jesus.

And maybe one does not usually fully understand all the ramifications of their new life in Christ after they accept Him as Savior. At least I didn't; and considering 60% of believers accept Christ when they are under the age of 14, I would say most do not fully understand. We hear the gospel as it is shared with us, and many feel led to accept this gracious gift. We recognize we are sinners, and know there is a void in our lives. We believe Christ died to pay for our sins, tell Him our need for Him, and fully believe what He has done for us.

"There is none righteous, not even one; there is none that understands, there is none who seeks for God; all have turned aside, together they have become useless; there is none who does good, there is not even one." Romans 3:10-12, Paul quotes from Psalm 14:1-3

We know God made a bridge for us to Him through Christ.

"For the wages of sin is death, but the free gift of God is eternal life in Christ Jesus our Lord." Romans 6:23

We know we need to acknowledge His gift and take the step of faith.

"... if you confess with your mouth that Jesus is Lord and believe in your heart that God raised Him from the dead, you will be saved; for with the heart a person believes, resulting in righteousness, and with the mouth he confesses, resulting in salvation. For the Scripture says, 'Whoever believes in Him will not be disappointed." Romans 10:9-11

"For whoever will call on the name of the Lord will be saved." Romans 10:13

There you have it folks. The Gospel plain and simple.

He chose you and He chose me and drew me to Himself.

There are demarcation points in our ongoing journey that change our lives forever. When I was thirteen I accepted Christ as my Savior. Then life began anew. I felt a peace. He loved me so much to choose me, but life was still challenging as I was a teenage girl who was going through many hardships I did not understand. And even though I wanted to grow, and loved studying God's Word, I had such a difficult time understanding His love for me and really… anyone's love for me.

1 Thessalonians tells us,

"Now may the God of peace Himself sanctify you entirely; and may your spirit and soul and body be preserved complete, without blame at the coming of our Lord Jesus Christ." I Thessalonians 5:23

The apostle Paul closes out his letter to the church in Thessalonica by acknowledging that God is the source of our sanctification. It is not in our own power to do anything to be sanctified. Only God Himself can separate us from sin to holiness. Paul uses the word "complete". We are made complete - Spirit and soul.

> *"Now to Him who is able to do far more abundantly beyond all that we ask or think, according to the power that works within us, to Him be the glory in the church and in Christ Jesus to all generations forever and ever. Amen." Ephesians 3:20-21*

God is so powerful, and He works in us beyond what we can understand. It is HIM doing it and not ourselves. At times we are reminded of this, especially when we see evidence of something remarkable that He has done in our lives.

I have a few testimonies throughout this book from people I admire for their strong faith. They have been challenged throughout their life, and God has worked through it all. I hope you are encouraged to trust our mighty God through hearing from these saints. The first one is from my friend Melanie. She grew up in Washington like myself, and has a very heartfelt journey to share.

> *I was born into familial alcoholism, and at about age 4 I began to realize that my father had serious issues with addiction which affected our lives. Because my parent's marriage was volatile, they sent me to my Grandparents for extended visits on Spring and Summer break. I had attended a Bible-teaching church very sporadically, but not enough to understand the Gospel of Good News. At age 7, I was staying with grandparents in Oregon who attended a Bible-teaching church. One day I was looking at a picture of Jesus, and my Grandmother asked me questions about how I felt about Jesus. That day, on her sewing stool she led me through the path of salvation by grace, and I prayed the sinner's prayer that day. I was saved that day, but God's hand and protection over me from that day on proved His Sovereignty in a vast way.*

I began attending a Bible teaching church as a teenager after moving to Idaho, and became involved with the youth group. A youth pastor began a Bible study, and gave me a deep understanding of carnality, and what an "infant" Christian I was. I'm so grateful for that study in 1 Corinthians! Christmas of 1973 my Dad's drinking became so violent that I had him arrested, and I didn't see him or have a relationship with him for 8 years.

In 1976 I was on my own, due to my mom's emotional breakdown and the absence of my father. God supernaturally and lovingly protected me during that year despite bad decisions and complete immaturity. God powerfully showed his care for me when I married my high school sweetheart in 1977, who was a believer. We were too young, and broke, but looking back, God's plans and purpose were steadfast! As a young wife, mom and college student, I attended a bible study taught by Ruthanne Beddoe, who was my Pastor's wife, and an incredible Godly woman and teacher. Her lessons made me hungry and excited for Bible study, and the Holy Spirit began changing me and working in my life in a powerful way.

More than four decades later, I still find everything I need and desire in His Word. It illuminates, gives me hope, and lights my way every moment of every day. As tests, trials, heartache, hardships, and brokenness have peppered my life since I placed my faith in Him, I pray He continues to purify me for His purpose. "I have fought the good fight, I have finished the course, I have kept the faith." 2 Tim 4:7

Melanie

This is an amazing story of God continually guiding Melanie through her many trials, and drawing her to Himself. He faithfully showed her that He held her in His arms, and knew her through and through. He was creating in her an empathetic heart that listens and cares. She has a soft heart for others and is continually ministering to many.

This makes me think of the disciples and the apostle Paul. They instantly followed and began serving. Did they have doubts? Did they clearly see all God would have for them? Luke tells us in Acts 26:18, that Jesus told Paul that He would use him.

> *"to open their eyes so that they may turn from darkness to light, and from the dominion of Satan to God, that they may receive forgiveness of sins and an inheritance among those who have been sanctified by faith in Me."*

Here the Apostle Paul is letting King Agrippa know that he has a choice to turn from darkness to light. In previous verses Paul tells the King that he had locked up believers, but God chose him to serve Him even after all he had done. Can you imagine persecuting Christians, then serving the Lord who the very people you were persecuting worshiped?

Paul knew that if Agrippa did believe the prophets, then that should lead him to believe in Jesus. Don't we want that for everyone around us? Paul preaches Christ's Lordship hoping that those listening would see their need. Jesus told Paul that he was to open the eyes of the spiritually blind so they could walk from darkness into light. The Bible teaches us that over and over again that our salvation comes from God and not from works. We must have faith in God alone.

We too are given instructions in God's Word on how we are to live, and also how to serve. But one thing is for sure. You must start a new life in Him as Melanie points out in her testimony, and the Apostle Paul is one of the greatest examples of a new life in Christ.

*"An unveiling of atoning affection
Dazzling verifiable redemption
Set apart for the childlike heart"*

- Roger Saunders

CHAPTER TWO

Faith Rising

"In the same way the Spirit also helps our weakness; for we do not know how to pray as we should, but the Spirit Himself intercedes for us with groanings too deep for words; and He who searches the hearts knows what the mind of the Spirit is, because He intercedes for the saints according to the will of God."

ROMANS 8:26-27

Growing up on a horse ranch was fun sometimes but also a bit isolating. We lived in an old house that my moma swore had been a chicken coop. It was long and narrow with a door at each end. It had no windows on one side and the roof always leaked. There were many areas in the house that were not finished. My bedroom had insulation showing on two walls, as there was only paneling on the other two walls, not all four. I put posters up to decorate in an attempt to cover up the exposed insulation. I had no closet, just a metal pole to hold my clothes. Moma was ashamed of our house.Consequently, we never were allowed to have friends over. Our farm had 3,000 feet of riverfront, and one of the best swimming holes.

Our neighborhood friends consisted of those who lived across the river from us. In the summer we would swim with them, and sometimes they would help with the haying. This was great fun.

Because we had few friends, we became very involved in the youth group at church. What a blessing that was! We took full advantage of it. Our youth leaders and the other kids really motivated me to learn about God, and when I saw that they were always memorizing Scripture I joined in. I also learned about missionaries for the first time through a slide show, and decided I might become a missionary.

I think now that being at church was a great escape for me. It was a place where I could catch glimpses of positive things. I was not at home where life was hard: where the three of us survived on the $90 a month we received from Social Security. At the time, I did not even realize anything about how financially burdening this was for Moma. We also had rats in our house part of the time and Moma would pound on the walls with the broom when she heard them running through the walls. Otherwise, she was depressed and slept most afternoons but at that age I did not fully understand why she was sleeping all the time. I wish I could have asked someone. I am sure she was grieving, and feeling an immense amount of pressure not knowing what would happen to us. But then she always handed us a dollar to put into the offering at church each week.

God was working in her heart too although as a teen I could not see it.

I am so very thankful for our pastor who asked my sister, Lisa, and me to babysit their kids. We did not live that close to their home, and he might have been able to find someone who lived closer, but they chose us.

We looked forward to it, and it was a little bit of money we could have for ourselves. Our church also had my moma help with the church bookkeeping. I really believe this gave her a sense of worth.

We were never made to feel like we were needy, but I am sure people saw our need.

Reflecting on this part of my childhood now, I see how the church stepped up. It's not uncommon to hear disgruntled people talk about how their church never visited them when they were in the hospital, or how the people from the church never do anything for them. But ours did.

The church took care of us in the true definition of what the church should be.

While times were hard, I can see now how we were still growing and learning about God. Baby steps. Learning the Bible, with Christian friends encouraging us and praying for us. These are key elements that the body of Christ uses to nurture fellow believers.

Once again it is not like we are instantly perfect Christians. It is a process, and all these components help the body of Christ grow. 2 Peter 3:18 says,

"But grow in the grace and knowledge of our Lord Jesus Christ."

Peter wanted believers to understand about growing, and about the end times as he closes out his second letter. He is urging believers to be righteous, and diligent, and not complacent. If we are growing, then our mind is focused on giving God praise, and on our pursuit of godliness. Seeking maturity in Christ and a deepening knowledge of our Lord Jesus Christ will lead us to stable faith and prevent us from being led astray.

First and Second Peter are two of my most favorite books of the entire Bible. The first letter encourages believers who are suffering. And the second epistle concentrates on telling believers to be aware of false teachers. As believers mature in their faith, they should be able to discern if someone is teaching the truth or not. Shortly after that book was written Peter was martyred.

Paul also teaches us over and over about being strong in our faith. To become blameless, and to understand who God is and what He has intended for us.

I cannot really grasp how Paul felt after he became a believer after persecuting Christians for so long. I think I would feel so much remorse I would not be able to function, but he moved forward in the plan God had for him. He walked for miles, and travelled miles and miles by boat, and did what God instructed him. He then wrote letters from prison to continue to encourage believers in their faith. Wow.

I love these verses Paul gives us in his letter to the church at Colossae.

> *"For it was the Father's good pleasure for all the fullness to dwell in Him, and through Him to reconcile all things to Himself, having made peace through the blood of His cross; through Him, I say, whether things on earth or things in heaven. And although you were formerly alienated and hostile in mind, engaged in evil deeds, yet He has now reconciled you in His fleshly body through death, in order to present you before Him holy and blameless and beyond reproach—if indeed you continue in the faith firmly established and steadfast, and not moved away from the hope of the gospel that you have heard, which was proclaimed in all creation under heaven, and of which I, Paul, was made a minister. Colossians 1:19-23*

We are reconciled to Christ who died on the cross for us. "Reconciled" means "to bridge the gap."

Jesus bridged the gap, and restored our relationship with God through His death on the cross. We have Christ to help us persevere in our faith and obedience because we have been made righteous. Paul was concerned about young believers being swayed by false teachers.

But if we have a firm foundation in what we believe, then we will not be led away from the gospel and will continue to follow Jesus.

Another testimony that I want to share with you is from Spencer.

Spencer is a great example of an amazing young man who keeps moving forward on the path God has put him on, despite doubts and questions. He leads music, writes and performs songs, and has ministered in many ways at various churches and ministries. He also has an album out. Although I have been involved with music in many ways through the years, I am not an accomplished musician, but I relate to Spencer. I too am a creative person with a hundred ideas popping into my head at all times. And with that personality, I think it can lead us to also doubt and wonder. God made all personalities, and we are fearfully and wonderfully made, but some of us need more reassurance of this than others! There are positives, and things that may not seem as positive at the time, but they are for a purpose. God does not make mistakes. And with our weaknesses, He is faithful in directing us to the correct path if we continue to follow Him.

"But his delight is in the law of the Lord, and on his law he meditates day and night. He is like a tree planted by streams of water that yields its fruit in its season, and its leaf does not wither. In all that he does, he prospers." Psalm 1:2-3 (ESV)

"No matter how much I meditated on God's words, waves of doubt drowned my faith and confidence. Was this psalm even true? I should have displayed towering faith, especially with my upbringing. I was expertly homeschooled by two marriage and family counselor parents, my Bible was filled with notes and papers from Church, Sunday school, youth group, and anything else Christian I could attend. When anyone asked about my faith, I declared "I follow Jesus" but in my heart, I hid a darker truth, the reality of doubt, fear, and endless questions.

Why does God allow us to suffer? Why do so many people never trust in Jesus? Are they all going to hell, and if so, how is that fair? Did the universe just pop into existence? Does evolutionary theory disprove God's existence? How could I ever know if I had enough faith to be saved?

My mind grasped for answers. I buried the doubts in countless "salvation prayers" but I never felt "saved." As I studied Christian apologetics, glimmers of hope cut through the fog. The biblical worldview charted a route through my confusion, but somehow clouds always returned. It was like the Grand Canyon stood between my feet and the answers. A biblical perspective nearly bridged the gap, but couldn't answer every question. Other world views, whether atheistic, Buddhist, or Islamic left me stranded on the near side. Even though Christian arguments were the most convincing, I couldn't stop shooting holes in them.

Exhausted from the search for answers, I slumped to my bedroom floor and glued my eyes on the ceiling.

"God, if you're really who you say in the Bible, then you want me to believe in you. I've tried to have faith, but every time I get a little, it's not enough. I can't! You need to help me!"

Before my words could reflect off the dark ceiling, warmth wrapped me like an aggressive, but comforting hug. My frustration turned to unexplained peace, leaving me with no rational explanation other than God's presence. When my intellectual answers fell short, God proved to me that His power doesn't come from lofty arguments, but from His very Spirit.

From that moment I vowed to trust God when a prayer was answered, or I saw Him work, rather than explaining it as pure coincidence. Making that small commitment of faith exploded into seeing God's hand move everywhere: in my heart, fighting my own sin, in my youth group, at church camp, and beyond. Even though my faith would fluctuate over the years, Jesus meeting me in my bedroom sparked a flame that's grown ever since. I'll truly never be the same, and neither will you, just give him your small faith and he'll do the rest.

Spencer

When I first read Spencer's testimony I thought, Wow! He hit the nail on the head. Exactly what this book is about. Like Spencer I wondered how I could doubt God, but yet sometimes I did. Did this make sense? If you've ever had doubts about God or God's plan for you, just talk to Him, and He can expand your faith too.

"But God is the God of the waves and the billows, and they are still His when they come over us; and again and again we have proved that the overwhelming thing does not overwhelm. Once more by His interposition deliverance came. We were cast down, but not destroyed."

- Amy Carmichael

CHAPTER THREE

Rescued

"Because I delivered the poor who cried for help,
And the orphan who had no helper.
The blessing of the one ready to perish came upon me,
and I made the widow's heart sing for joy."
Job 29:12-13

As a newer believer I wanted everyone to know Christ. I mean, I just assumed everyone would want to. I would call everyone on our youth group list every Sunday to tell them to come; not really sure what I thought that would do, but I was just excited. Some of them did not really want to come. I did not understand that, but then church was sort of an escape for me. It was the most positive thing I had in my life at the time.

Times were difficult at home when I was in high school. I think about it now, and how sad my moma must have been, not just because dad died, but because she did not know how to pay the taxes or where food would come from. A year after our dad died, our grandma died. Dad and Grandma Anna Mae were the foundation of our family. They had always been the ones to make decisions and plans. They were my moma's foundation, and now they were gone. Moma remained faithful to going to church, and making sure we were ok, but she slept every afternoon, and I could tell she was struggling mentally. I found her crying one day, and I asked her why, and she told me she had to ask our grandpa to pay the taxes ... again.

She clearly did not want to do this. Grandpa Archie was a quiet man, he did not say much. And although he knew Moma was suffering, he was not someone she could lean on for support. I am so thankful that he helped Moma out in the ways that he was able. He ate meals with us, and worked outside on our farm, keeping up much of the flower beds and barn area. Moma prayed for him, and years later she led him to Christ as he was dying.

I look back now, and think I could have been more supportive to her, but I was so into my own survival, I could not see that. I do not remember exactly which year, but at one point, Lisa and I realized we had to do something about all the cats in our house. In addition to our few pet cats, there were feral cats living in dark corners of the house. They were wild and extremely difficult to catch because they were not used to human contact. We might have had 16 to 20 cats, or maybe more, inside the house. They'd taken over. Our house smelled, and we could not feed them all.... I'm grimacing now as I think about that. So we had to do what no teenage girls should have to do. It was a terrible day I'll never forget. We carried gunny sacks, put a cat inside, and drowned it in the horse trough. We did this over and over, then buried them in the field by the barn. It was so difficult, but necessary. Lisa had to take charge because Moma was not able to cope at the time. I just learned recently that Lisa had to do this multiple times because we did not catch all the cats that first day. She also took her beloved orange tiger stripe cat, Tommy, to town one day and dropped him off in a neighborhood hoping that someone would take him in.

To those of you out there thinking you'd never do such a thing, let me tell you: There are millions of hurting people in the world who have to do hard things for survival.

Moma never acknowledged what we were doing. She stayed in the house and none of us ever spoke of it. Ever. As the oldest, Lisa had to deal with most of the problems. Moma was so overwhelmed by grief, circumstances, our home, everything - she was beyond wanting to face reality. God rescued Lisa and I. We may not have understood at the time, but He gave us hope in Him.

Life on our farm was so difficult. There was always something that needed to be done. I can remember, once, digging a fence post hole in the pouring rain. Standing, soaking wet, with tears running down my face, praying someone would stop by to help. They didn't that day, but there were many times someone did check on my Moma, and helped us out. I am so very thankful.

Why do I tell you this? What does this have to do with growing in Christ? Each one of us has experiences or obstacles that are seared into our brain forever, and they serve as lessons much later in life. You can experience tragedy, learn something, or overhear a conversation as a child that stays with you forever, and it is these experiences that give us empathy for others.

I learned more from a childhood of adversity than anything else, and I will always strive to help others less fortunate because of it. Be aware of those around you who may be on the fringe in your community or at your church, those who are hurting. Do you know their stories? Have you checked in on them? Is there someone that God wants you to reach out to, to give them hope and God's love? Often it's just a simple act of kindness that can change everything.

James 1:27 states,

> *"Pure and undefiled religion in the sight of our God and Father is this: to visit orphans and widows in their distress, and to keep oneself unstained by the world."*

This is practical faith. Our faith involves actively caring for others, especially those in need. God is concerned for those in need. Caring for widows and orphans is a sacrificial type of love because they most generally would not be able to reciprocate.

> *"He executes justice for the orphan and the widow, and shows His love for the alien by giving him food and clothing." Deuteronomy 10:18*

I am so very thankful for our little church. I did not understand then, but I know people in that church loved us and prayed for us regularly. The body of Christ is so important. It is our connection. God uses others in our life, and can use us too. As someone who was in great need, I felt rescued. Still needy in physical ways, but spiritually rescued. God was watching out for us, and as time went by, I could see there was a plan. I could see Him leading us through the rough waters, and into the safety of His plan for us.

As time wore on, and I was getting closer to the end of high school, I realized that I needed to flee to a mentally healthy place. I thought that would make everything all better. So I trudged along during the last couple years of high school - even though I actually loved school. I was able to go to many fun places with our youth group, played tennis at school, was an ASB officer, in German club, choir and painted a mural on the library wall. These things all helped me move forward in life. I am sure most people did not know I struggled so much, except my closest friends. I was fairly popular, always in student government, but I hid out in the German classroom often at lunch because I was concerned no one would want to hang out with me. Not really victorious living. Had I truly understood that I was complete in Christ, maybe I wouldn't have struggled so much.

But then again, it's the struggle that acts as a kaleidoscope, isn't it? You can relate to the struggles others are facing perhaps because you struggled with something similar when you were younger. Your struggle is different than mine, and mine will be different than the next person.

My high school experience wasn't always comfortable yet, God was working in ways I did not even realize.

Decades later, I have had former classmates tell me how much they appreciated me in high school because I always greeted them or was kind. They tell me how I was so popular but always took time for them. HA. I am shocked at their glowing remembrances of me, because I was a mess! But I am glad I showed some of them I cared. I know those who knew me best knew how much I struggled.

My sister, who was two years older than me, went away to college, which was a very somber day yet also one that made me so happy. She was free. She was in God's hands and He had given her direction.

I had two more years until I too could go. I am so very thankful I had friends around me, and did not know at the time how many people were looking out for us. What a blessing it is for God to use others in your life.

I had a wonderful Christian best friend at school, and others too who knew I had hard times. I had two girls come down to the farm and ask Moma if they could take me to a movie. She said yes! They took me to dinner and a movie too, and no one had ever done that for me before. It was a wonderful evening. Befriending someone in need is a wonderful thing. I was the recipient of many such actions, and it made all the difference in my life. There were also people who helped my mother, who was now a widow.

God shapes us through our life's circumstances and even today I am continually burdened for widows and orphans. I am certain it was my own circumstance as an adoptee, who lived with a widowed mom, that created this deep compassion.

Your experiences in childhood shape you, and yet God sees it all. The things that you had to endure, whether it was on the playground, in the classroom, or at home, made you stronger, and who you are. If you had to suffer the loss of a parent or even watch someone in your family struggle, that shaped you too.

Moma was very passive aggressive. At night in the house it was so much emptier without my sister there.

Moma never yelled or was mean in an overt way. At least not that I recall. But the quiet control was driving me mad. Seriously. I remember peeling potatoes for dinner one night and she was just quietly saying that I was not a nice person and on and on. Listening to her criticize me, I peeled my finger, on purpose. She was standing behind me and said, "go ahead Nicki peel your finger." She was mentally ill. Depression had overtaken her. Part of me felt sorry for her and part of me wanted to run far away.

When I finally did, I went to college. It was the same small Christian college that Lisa attended. Of course I knew I would be back on breaks, but college was my first real taste of freedom.

Moma would call at 7 a.m. on Saturday mornings, unfortunate since there was only one phone in our hall and the person living next to the phone had to answer it and then come get me. Then Moma would just talk for a minute, "I hope you are having a nice life, Nicki". Then hang up. Very quietly throwing a tiny spear. Perhaps it was her way of dealing with the loneliness, by venting her anger at all of it.

At times I would go stand under a gutter spout during a L.A. rainstorm and let the rain pour over me. My dorm RA (hall manager) one time told me that she had seen similar behavior from my sister, Lisa, who had also lived on campus. We were a mess. BUT GOD was with us through it all.

My favorite thing to do is to read the book of Psalms. Especially those written by David, but I love them all. Why? Because David yells at God and tells his heartbreak, then by the end of the Psalm he praises God. David shares his thoughts and emotions with God. He tells Him everything. Not that God does not already know, but God wants us to share our heart with Him. I read Psalms over and over. I underline and write notes. It comforts me more than anything. About 20 years ago I was reading Psalm 37. This is a popular Psalm. It tells us to trust the Lord and not to be anxious when we see wicked people prosper. BUT all of a sudden I noticed verses 23-24. How did I miss these promises?

"The steps of a man are established by the LORD, and He delights in his way. When he falls, he will not be hurled headlong, ***because the LORD is the one who holds his hand."***

Oh my. I had a new set of life verses. I have shared this over and over with others. Divine comfort. God will never let me go. EVER. And He won't let go of you either. The path may be rocky, dear believer, but He is right there.

"My eyes are continually toward the LORD, For He will pluck my feet out of the net." Psalm 25:15

Keep your eyes upward. He will take you out of the snare you are caught in. He will rescue you from your situation that you may think is hopeless. But then it is a new day and you can see the plan along your journey. And you can see how He has brought you out of it and once again you are rescued.

"In EVERY situation and EVERY circumstance of your life, God is always doing a thousand different things that you cannot see and you do not know."

- John Piper

CHAPTER FOUR

Forget the Mess

Brethren, I do not regard myself
as having laid hold of it yet;
but one thing I do: forgetting what lies behind
and reaching forward to what lies ahead,
I press on toward the goal for the prize
of the upward call of God in Christ Jesus.
PHILIPPIANS 3:13-14

It is easy to focus on the here and now, with life going on all around you.

It is harder to focus on helping others, especially if you can't see the invisible struggles they're dealing with.

Yet we are all commanded to love.

> *"This is My commandment, that you love one another, just as I have loved you. Greater love has no one than this, that one lay down his life for his friends." John 15:12-13*

Jesus is telling us to love others. Again. It is easy to get wrapped up with our own problems, and there are many people around us going through intense trials. I try to tune in to those who are hurting. I can take a meal, give them a call, or send them a note. Later in life, my moma wrote to people every week. She would draw little pictures of birds and flowers, and mail them to people. At her funeral, someone mentioned that she got weekly notes from Moma, even though she lived only a few miles away. What fun it is to receive a letter in the mail from someone saying they cared. We can all do spontaneous things for those around us. It does not always need to be monetary, just a walk, or sit on the porch and visit, something to show them they are thought of and loved.

When I was attending college, I was amazed to realize that I still had to work through some of the same issues I thought would disappear when I left home. I was so thankful to be surrounded by other kids who loved God and showed love to me. Many of them came from solid homes where they had been loved and encouraged. They shared Bible verses with me. One of the most influential passages to me was from Philippians chapter 3, verses 7-14:

> *"But whatever things were gain to me, those things I have counted as loss for the sake of Christ. More than that, I count all things to be loss in view of the surpassing value of knowing Christ Jesus my Lord, for whom I have suffered the loss of all things, and count them but rubbish so that I may gain Christ, and may be found in Him, not having a righteousness of my own derived from the Law, but that which is through faith in Christ, the righteousness which comes from God on the basis of faith, that I may know Him and the power of His resurrection and the fellowship of His sufferings, being conformed to His death; in order that I may attain to the resurrection from the dead. Not that I have already obtained it or have already become perfect, but I press on so that I may lay hold*

of that for which also I was laid hold of by Christ Jesus. Brethren, I do not regard myself as having laid hold of it yet; but one thing I do: forgetting what lies behind and reaching forward to what lies ahead, I press on toward the goal for the prize of the upward call of God in Christ Jesus."

For the first time I really grasped the idea that I was not to be chained to my past, but I was chosen to be more like Christ. Everything I was dwelling on was rubbish - garbage! My righteousness was not based on who and what I had been, but on my faith in Christ. At the end of this passage, it tells me to forget what lies behind and press on to be more like Christ. Wow. What an awakening for me. I claimed that as a life verse. It wasn't like I was instantly perfect, or that life was easy, but I knew that I did not have to be stuck in my past, but God would help me move forward. To be stuck in the past hinders one's ability to move forward. Not only should we not dwell on past failures but we also should not rely on past accomplishments. We need to move forward, and concentrate on what God has for us to do now. Today. This week.

This book is a gentle reminder on the process of sanctification. The pursuit of Christlikeness. We can take steps toward this goal. Verse 14 refers to our eternal goal. The ultimate goal. When we are in Christ's presence.

Isaiah 43:18-19 tells us,

"Do not call to mind the former things or ponder things of the past. Behold, I will do something new, now it will spring forth; will you not be aware of it? I will even make a roadway in the wilderness, rivers in the desert."

Whoa! What an amazing concept. God is telling His people that He is creating a new life for them. God will overcome all the obstacles and provide sustenance for us. He transforms us and gives us hope for the future. Not only did God take care of our past, but He promises deliverance for us now and in the future.

The apostle Paul tells us in 2 Corinthians 5:17,

> *"Therefore if anyone is in Christ, he is a new creature; the old things passed away; behold, new things have come."*

We have a relationship with God that we did not possess before. We are no longer separated from God, but we are transformed. We are entirely new in our transformation, and take on a new identity. It does not mean, however, that life will be without struggles or hardship. I think it is common thinking amongst new believers that life will be less difficult. They may even get disillusioned from hardship they are still going through. But remember, God does not necessarily take difficult things away, but He gives us hope as we go through them. Things will not always be perfect. But God is molding us into who He designed us to be.

> *But now, oh LORD, You are the Father, we are the clay, and You are the potter; and all of us are the work of Your hand." Isaiah 64:5-8*

When I was a sophomore in college, I had a friend, Steve, who took pity on a fatherless girl who seemed insecure and messed up. I was so very thankful for Steve, who helped me buy my first car: a '68 Cougar 302, 4-barrel, with Crager mags and air shocks. Not sure it was the most sensible car for me…who was already a bit rowdy, but I was so very thankful to have a car. This is one of the many things Steve helped me with that summer as I lived on campus over the break. I had nowhere to go. I went home for a week, but did not feel I could stay there the entire summer. Having a solid friend was a great encouragement to me.

In recent years, I have become better acquainted with his sister, Karen, and her husband, Jim. I tell you, that family was raised right. They are always caring for others before themselves. Selfless service for God. They are on my ministry team, and I am so fortunate to know them. Here is a testimony from Karen. She has gone through much pain but shines for her Lord.

40 years ago I was a mess. I was in a deep depression.

I grew up in Southern California near Los Angeles Baptist College, where I went to school and met my husband, Jim. We were married in 1980. Jim was youth pastor at Valley Baptist Church in Burbank at that time. A few months into our marriage, my Dad died suddenly, and the shock was overwhelming. Somehow through all the shock, I knew God still cared about our family. Somehow we thought we would be okay. We thought being a Christian would make going through it easier. Wrong! We are still human and grief hits regardless.

About 18 months later, Jim was asked to candidate at a church in Montana. So we went up in May 1982 to spend time getting to know the folks. It was good, so different though. One couple we went on a picnic with told us, as they let us off at our host's home, "Be sure to check for ticks!" What?!? I guess it is Montana! So at the end of 2 weeks the folks voted to call Jim as their pastor. So we headed home to pack, and tell our church family we were leaving.

Two months later we were all packed up, driving a Ryder truck towing our little VW. Excited and scared. We arrived in Montana a few days later, and we settled into our basement apartment and began to get into the work of the church.

I tended to be timid, and an introvert, and it was hard to get to know folks well. I was afraid I would not be a perfect Christian, or a perfect wife, or a perfect pastor's wife....just having been a wife for only 2 1/2 years, and just beginning being a pastor's wife! I didn't know how.

Difficult things happened. Family so far away, missing them but not thinking I should feel sad, relatives dying, losing friends who moved away when I had just begun to know them well, Jim spending so much time with the church work....I was getting lost even though I was involved with music and teaching kids. Just not adjusting, and still grieving for Dad - only I didn't realize that at the time. So when my grandmother got cancer, and my Mom went to stay to take care of her, and I could not talk with her much....and some materials came in the mail from Life Action Ministries about Revival....really talking about real things I realize I needed...I began crying (I never cried) every day and much of the day. I started realizing I was studying my Sunday School lesson to teach, instead of having quiet time alone with Jesus. And I didn't know Him very well at all. Not well enough to go through these hard things.

Well as time went on, a pastor counseled me, one who shared his own times of depression, and God's Spirit began to do the work of showing me how much God loved me. He loved me even though I wasn't the perfect Christian, or perfect wife, or perfect pastor's wife.... for a while I didn't even believe God much. This pastor believed for me. But one day Mormon missionaries came to the door, and I realized that they did not know the Truth, I did: the Lord Jesus Christ and His Word! That took care of it for me, the road back began to get brighter, and the depression began to get lighter. It helped that the Life Action ministry came to our church, and helped us with getting back to the truths of admitting sin, confessing, repenting, making restitution, having an accountability partner, and more.

The pastor had me write out certain Scriptures on 3x5 cards. I was to read them over 4 times a day. They didn't make much sense at first, but as the days went on they got into my heart.

Music was such a help during the time of depression. I had certain records that I played over and over.... the Christian influence got deep inside to help me...40 years later I still know the tunes and many of the words.

A couple things happened that others noticed. My music had been quite perfectly in time....but not much expression. After the time of depression, the expression from my heart began to come out in the music. I could feel it for the first time. And I began to care about people, really care what happened to them. I don't think I really did before that.

It also really helped that I had a couple of ladies in the church that I could talk openly to. I had not been very real or open before, but I learned to not worry so much about what other people think. What God thinks is what matters! When I admitted to our church family that I was struggling with depression, immediately a lady who was in our church who had struggled a long time with depression, felt like she could talk to me as I finally could understand.

Grieving losses is ok....and it is ok to not be perfect....I couldn't be any way! God helped me not be so hard on myself and let me grow. I have not arrived, and have a long way to go, and sometimes it is three steps forward two steps back, but God keeps working on me.

Karen

Karen moved forward in what God intended for her life. She ministers to all those around her. Yes, we are all a work in progress. God doesn't give up on us. Sometimes it is easy to be filled with an over-occupation with feelings of the past or self-pity, but we can be free from that, beloved. Trust God. Be healed. God is using your hard time to mold you and make you into His instrument.

"When we are confident in our identity in Christ, then our true selves – our God-given personalities, gifts, and passions – can shine bright."

- Jessica Faith Hagen

CHAPTER FIVE

Who You Are

"But you are a chosen race, a royal priesthood, a holy nation, a people for God's own possession, so that you may proclaim the excellencies of Him who has called you out of darkness into His marvelous light; for you once were not a people, but now you are the people of God; you had not received mercy, but now you have received mercy."

I PETER 2:9-10

I began studying Ephesians and learned that God chose us and predestined us.

> *"Blessed be the God and Father of our Lord Jesus Christ, who has blessed us with every spiritual blessing in the heavenly places in Christ, just as He chose us in Him before the foundation of the world, that we would be holy and blameless before Him. In love He predestined us to adoption as sons through Jesus Christ to Himself, according to the kind intention of His will, to the praise of the glory of His grace, which He freely bestowed on us in the Beloved." Ephesians 1:3-6*

That meant God chose ME. And no one could take that away.

Now it was time to move on to what God had planned for me. During my sophomore year in college, I changed my major from Education to Biblical Studies. The head of the Education department thought I was nuts. He asked, "What was a woman going to do with a Bible major?" I told him that my education major classes were boring to me, and that my favorite classes were my Bible classes. I did not really think about jobs at that point, and I did end up subbing for 12 years later in life, but I loved my Bible classes. I did not have a long term plan, it just didn't matter to me. I sat and soaked up all the information I could. If God had called me to share the gospel and teach others about God, how could I go wrong?

Upper division bible classes were tough for me. There were hardly any other women, and there were older seminary students in some of my classes. Living in Southern California, and being an artsy free-spirit type of person, and sort of a beach bum, I am sure I did not fit the mold. But somehow I actually felt embraced by my professors. They knew my grades, my life struggles, and somehow I felt I was a favorite. I'm not sure if that was true, but I embraced this path I was on. Approaching graduation, I realized I had no plan, and I knew I did not want to go home. While I knew God wanted me to serve Him, I still struggled with so much hurt. I tried to not let the baggage of my growing up years weigh me down, but there was that corner of my life I had not overcome. Little did I know that my Bible professors understood my heartbreak. I think they knew our home situation the entire time, and they formed a plan. They asked me to be secretary for the Bible department. I was stoked! Somehow I thought of this as a "safe spot" for me. I would be surrounded by people who could keep me on God's path. I still did not understand that change comes from within, not from outside circumstances.

I had never been a secretary before, but hey, I could use a typewriter (this was before the age of computers), and had taken Greek and understood the classes. My heart was hurting, as my grandpa Archie had died a few months later. I did not have money to go home for the funeral. I was broken for my moma who would now be alone on the farm. Years later, my sister told me that she found a journal where our moma wrote that Moma was in a very dark place. That next summer when I went home, there was a piece of paper taped onto the fridge that said, "No one can make me angry but myself." Wow. God was working on Moma too.

There are a few Bible passages that are my favorites that remind me how much God cares and strengthens us.

"Do not fear, for I am with you; Do not anxiously look about you, for I am your God. I will strengthen you, surely I will help you, surely I will uphold you with My righteous right hand." Isaiah 41:10

And also,

"God is our refuge and strength, a very present help in trouble. Therefore we will not fear, though the earth should change and though the mountains slip into the heart of the sea." Psalm 46:1-2

God chose me and other believers before the foundation of the world for His purposes. He may choose to bring you through a storm to grow you. But He is still with you in the storm. He is there listening to us and keeping watch over us. He will not allow us to go under. Psalm 46 addresses the adequacy of God. He protects His people on earth, and we need not fear. This psalm is also the inspiration for Martin Luther's beautiful hymn, "A Mighty Fortress Is Our God."

A mighty fortress is our God, a bulwark never failing;
Our helper He, amid the flood of mortal ills prevailing:
For still our ancient foe doth seek to work us woe;

His craft and pow'r are great, and, armed with cruel hate,
On earth is not his equal.

Understanding who we are, and that no matter what happens, He loves us and is with us. This is His desire for each of us. It may take time but He is continually growing us. As He prunes us, He grants us all His blessings, and directions in His Word.

I asked my college friend, Roger, to share about some of his life lessons that led him to maturing in Christ.

Some folks will tell you that you can't understand what it means to give your life to Jesus Christ as a small child.

However, I can remember that day with all of the sensory details as if it was this very morning. As my custom was, as a little boy just a couple of weeks short of my fourth birthday, I woke up, padded into my parent's bedroom, and crawled under the covers with my Mom. She explained the Gospel: from Adam and Eve until the Resurrection of our Lord. I knew I had sinned because I'd already hauled off and smacked my little brother who was 17 months younger. I knew I needed forgiveness. I asked Jesus to come into my heart and save me from my sin! It was definitely the faith of a small child, which only came by hearing the Word of God, as Jesus so simply put it.

However, this was only the beginning of learning how to relate to the one who saved my soul.

I was so blessed to be brought up in a home where two flawed people put their trust in God as well. But I was under the impression, over the next 40 years or so, that it had way more to do with what I had to do rather than what Jesus had done for me. I had no problem believing that I could not save myself at all, but I DID have the mistaken notion that it was me who did the giving of my heart instead of Him who gave me the gift of child-like faith. I needed to learn that while I was justified by His gift of faith, there was a growing process that could never take place unless He had chosen me, rather than I being the one who chose Him. I lived under the mistaken impression that if I could just live for Jesus, then my life would not encounter all of the pain that comes with having been born with a sin nature in a sinful world.

In the mid-40's of this mid-60's life of mine, I had to look back at the trouble I had gone through. A life of failed and unfinished business. My faith had not wavered but my choices had left a wake of regret and shame, as I felt as if I had not lived up to my part of the bargain of Salvation.

Unfinished education, two failed marriages, and unrealized dreams took me to a place where I actually became angry with myself and God. Hadn't I been loyal and unwavering in my faith? If so, WHY had so many things seemingly gone wrong in my life? Didn't God know how much faith I had put in Him? Why had life taken so many hurtful turns?

This began a journey, for me, that is still ongoing. Of course, the poor choices were my responsibility. I knew this in my heart, but the real turning point was when the reality of faith hit me. It was not MY faith. It was HIS gift! This further gift of insight that could only have come from the Holy Spirit, who DID live inside me.

Jesus used my troubles to finally have me hear the Truth. I was then given a beautiful gift that "restored the years the locusts had eaten." This is my wife of 14 years now.

But it was only the beginning of learning, that, "in this world we will face tribulation, but be not afraid ... For I, Jesus Christ, have overcome the world."

So NOW, my troubles have stopped!?!

Not a chance!

But through this process The Lord has been patient with me. and I am learning anew ... sometimes each hour of each day ... that my troubles are only a reminder that it's His powerful love that not only saved me but is using those troubles, as the ancient song writer says, "to mold me and make me after His will, while I am waiting, yielded and still."

I have found out that God is more patient with our "Why's" than we could ever imagine, and he uses "Be still and know that I am God" to sanctify us ... to set us apart ... for HIS will.

This is truly the one and only magnificent reason that we can consider it PURE JOY when we face various trials, because we know that the testing of our faith produces a perseverance that will complete the process of Sanctification, which will only end on that glorious day when we see Jesus face to face and heart to heart!

Roger

Roger, like myself, had many doubts. He questioned his hardships, but submitted to God's plan even though he knew there would still be trials.

The Bible tells us,

"... In the world you will have tribulation..." John 16:33.

We all have hard times. Are mine any worse than other people's? In Psalm 22:11 the psalmist requests from God,

"Be not far from me for trouble is near."

I believe as we mature we come to realize that our life will never be without hard times. It does not mean God does not love us. It is because He loves us and chose us, and is preparing us for more.

"For I consider that the sufferings of this present time are not worthy to be compared with the glory that is to be revealed to us." Romans 8:18

Do you wonder why you were made the way you are? With your specific family, with your personality, with your trials? I am an adopted woman so maybe I question things a bit more, especially why I was put into a family that would have so much hardship. That is actually the theme of my first book, "Not Really A Princess."

So many people questioned the title. As a believer in Christ, "You are a daughter of the King!" they would exclaim. But that is not what I meant by my book title. As an adopted person you sometimes wonder if life may have been different if you were raised by someone else or a birth parent, then you find out it would have been much worse. It was not better. I was **not really** a princess. Then you look over your life and you see the path God made, and you understand you are exactly where he put you for a reason. You are who He created you to be, and He will work through joys and hardships, for you to become who He wants you to be.

"Though our feelings come and go,
God's love for us does not."

- C. S. Lewis

CHAPTER SIX

Accept His Love

"See how great a love the Father has bestowed on us,
that we would be called children of God; and such we are.
For this reason the world does not know us,
because it did not know Him."
1 JOHN 3:1

Sometimes it is hard for believers to remain focused on God's love for us through our suffering or our feelings of unworthiness. We focus on the guilt, the hurt or the trial, but we need to understand that God does love us, and works in mysterious ways we may not understand.

Reading the Word of God, understanding who He is, and seeing over and over His faithfulness through thousands of years, shows me how much He loves believers.

I think Psalm 139 explains it the very best.

"O LORD, You have searched me and known me. You know when I sit down and when I rise up. You understand my thought from afar. You scrutinize my path and my lying down, and are inti-

mately acquainted with all my ways. Even before there is a word on my tongue, behold, O Lord, You know it all. You have enclosed me behind and before, and laid Your hand upon me. Such knowledge is too wonderful for me. It is too high, I cannot attain to it.

Where can I go from Your Spirit? Or where can I flee from Your presence? If I ascend to heaven, You are there. If I make my bed in Sheol, behold, You are there. If I take the wings of the dawn, if I dwell in the remotest part of the sea, even there Your hand will lead me, and Your right hand will lay hold of me. If I say, 'Surely the darkness will overwhelm me, and the light around me will be night,' even the darkness is not dark to You, and the night is as bright as the day. Darkness and light are alike to You.

For You formed my inward parts; You wove me in my mother's womb. I will give thanks to You, for I am fearfully and wonderfully made; Wonderful are Your works, and my soul knows it very well. My frame was not hidden from You, when I was made in secret, and skillfully wrought in the depths of the earth. Your eyes have seen my unformed substance; and in Your book were all written the days that were ordained for me, when as yet there was not one of them.

How precious also are Your thoughts to me, O God! How vast is the sum of them! If I should count them, they would outnumber the sand. When I awake, I am still with You.

O that You would slay the wicked, O God; Depart from me, therefore, men of bloodshed. For they speak against You wickedly, and Your enemies take Your name in vain. Do I not hate those who hate You, O Lord? And do I not loathe those who rise up against You? I hate them with the utmost hatred; They have become my enemies.

Search me, O God, and know my heart; Try me and know my anxious thoughts; And see if there be any hurtful way in me, and lead me in the everlasting way."

This Psalm of David shows how David is in awe of how closely and intimately God knows him. He knows God watches over him and that God planned out David's life before he was conceived.

How can I doubt God's love for me, His plan for me, when He knows me so well? He knows my path. He has given me a special purpose. He loves me. That is such an amazing thing.

God loves us no matter what we have done in the past. He loves us and is with us when we experience trials and difficulties in life. Accept God's love. Believe that He chose you - You, with all your flaws, hurts and inadequacies. This was something I did not learn for many years.

I love these verses in Philippians chapter one:

"And this I pray, that your love may abound still more and more in real knowledge and all discernment, so that you may approve the things that are excellent, in order to be sincere and blameless until the day of Christ; having been filled with the fruit of righteousness which comes through Jesus Christ, to the glory and praise of God." Philippians 1:9-11

Biblical love is very deeply rooted in scripture. It helps us to discern right from wrong and is not a false sentiment, but true and right. So it does not seem right for me not to accept that He loves me, when He wants me to abound and to be filled with His love and righteousness. The depth of God's love is vast and secure. Eternal. The most memorized Bible verse of all time tells us this.

"For God so loved the world that He gave His only begotten son, that whoever believes in Him shall not perish but have eternal life." John 3:16

God gave HIS ONLY SON. For me and you. That is an immense cost to demonstrate how very much He loves us. And if we fully know that God loves us, then we need to accept it. Otherwise, do we really know Him and who He is? Once we accept His love for us, then we see more clearly how we can love others. No matter who they are.

"Whoever does not love does not know God, because God is love." 1 John 4:8

Love is in us because we know God. And He shows us how to love others.

"Since you have in obedience to the truth purified your souls for a sincere love of the brethren, fervently love one another from the heart." 1 Peter 1:22

Fervently means to stretch to the limits. That is a whole lot of love. Once we fully understand how much He loves us, and how much we should love others, it is second nature to help people and show compassion to them and meet their needs.

The idea that we should love others is throughout the Bible - realize the power of these words:

"You shall not take vengeance, nor bear any grudge against the sons of your people, but you shall love your neighbor as yourself; I am the Lord." Leviticus 19:18

And again in Matthew 22:36-40,

"Teacher, which is the great commandment in the Law?' And He said to him, 'You shall love the Lord Your God with all your heart and with all your soul, and with all your mind. This is the great and foremost commandment. The second is like it, 'You shall love

your neighbor as yourself.' On these two commandments depend the whole law and the prophets."

These verses instruct believers to love others the same as they would love themselves. Not thinking of themselves as better, or any type of self love, but that they would see others through the lens of love: God's love for us and our love for others.

Actively choosing to show love for others, by being patient and kind, fills us with love. We build relationships with others. Sometimes I think it is easier to love others rather than believing He loves us and has a plan for us. Seeking God's presence by attending church, and participating in worship, encourages our heart and helps us to feel God's love for us. Spending time in prayer, talking with God, always draws me closer to Him. I have often written letters to God by keeping a journal. Writing prayers out helps you to reflect longer.

So what drives us onward? Do we trust Him to guide us? Do we believe with our whole heart that He will transform us into who He wants us to be? Or do we hold back because we see our sin as too great for Him? Do we truly believe that He can love us? As someone who has always struggled with acceptance, this was a real problem for me.

The Bible uses the term "justification," which is used to describe God's work in saving us from the penalty of sin, while "sanctification" refers to our salvation from the power of sin. I was freed from the penalty of sin when I was saved, but I kept trying to earn God's approval. And for years I wanted the approval of others too. I still have difficulty with cliques and feeling like I don't fit in or feeling left out. Perhaps our thorn is the tool that God uses to give us empathy and understanding, in our ministry to others.

I did believe He loved me, and saved me, and chose me. I did believe that He wanted me to serve Him, BUT I did not think that I could ever accomplish the great things others could - those who had grown up in loving Christian homes and who had been surrounded by godly people. I am so thankful that I no longer feel that way. I may still freeze when I walk into a room, and be nervous to sit down by someone, but that is not what God wants for me. And I know it. God has already granted me victory. It just took me a while to see it. Perhaps you also struggle with this? We are human, after all.

One of my best friends in college was very shy, and a very quiet, sweet person. Sort of the opposite of me. I so wanted to be like her. One day we were sitting in her dorm room, and I was telling her how everyone loved her, and that she was an example to me as a godly friend. She responded by telling me that being shy is actually selfish, because you are always thinking of yourself and not others. It is all about you, and how they may treat you. I was shocked, but now I can see her point. I can also see how me being overly concerned if others accept me is also selfish, and not how God wants me to be. He wants me to love others around me, and Him most of all. He wants me to be Christlike.

I saw an overview definition of what it means to be Christlike and it states, "to embody the qualities, character, and spirit of Jesus, not just as following His teachings but also reflecting His love, grace, humility, and service in daily life."

1 John 2:3-6 tells us,

> *"By this we know that we have come to know Him, if we keep His commandments. The one who says, "I have come to know Him," and does not keep His commandments, is a liar, and the truth is not in him; but whoever keeps His word, in him the love of God has truly been perfected. By this we know that we are in Him: the one who says he abides in Him ought himself to walk in the same manner as He walked."*

Obedience is a visible proof of God living in us. If we are a true believer, then that desire to obey and live for Him should reflect our belief. The apostle John uses the word, “know” 40 times in this epistle. Definitely a favorite of his. Why? Because it shows the genuineness of our faith. The assurance we have in Him. And if we are a true believer, we should be walking in the light and showing Christlikeness. I believe as we grow and obey, we start showing more love to others and the focus moves more off ourselves. This passage continues in verses 7-11,

> *“Brethren, I write no new commandment to you, but an old commandment which you have had from the beginning. Again a new commandment I write to you, which thing is true in Him and in you, because the darkness is passing away, and the true light is already shining. He who says he is in the light, and hates his brother, is in darkness until now. He who loves his brother abides in the light and there is no cause for stumbling in him. But he who hates his brother is in darkness and walks in darkness, and does not know where he is going, because the darkness has blinded his eyes.” 1 John 2:7-11*

Christians should be characterized by love. Thinking everything is all about us, or how someone is mistreating us, is not showing Christ to others. We all feel hurt or left out at times, but we must keep turning to who God wants us to be. Accept His love and live out His love. His Word is the best way to stay the course. It is our instruction book. It shows us who God is, and what His plan is for us. Study it and it will fill you up.

The last couple years of my moma’s life, I went back and forth from the Boise area to our farm in Western Washington more often than usual. I often felt sadness because I did not know if I would see her again. I recall the fall she was 97. She was definitely having a more difficult time. She was on Hospice care, and kept saying she did not understand why she was still around. She used to call everyone in her retiree group from church each morning and evening, but one by one they had passed away. I truly believe it wasn't about "her" but about the rest of us who remained. If you have no means and are home-bound…God can still use you my friend. You can still pray. And you can let others know they are loved, like Moma did. Years later people found journals and scraps of paper everywhere that she had written prayer requests on.

We all had been growing and changing. Lisa and her family lived in the other house on the farm and since she was a RN, she helped Moma every day. I did not see those day to day changes like Lisa did, as I only visited every few months. I was nervous to be alone with a frail 80 pound, 4 foot tall woman. And I still had scars. DECADES LATER, people would come and cry as they held her hand, and thanked her for praying for them and their teen. In my head I'd say, "but do you know who she really is?" But I was wrong…she was no longer the passive aggressive woman who would quietly say hurtful things. God had radically changed her. Praise God that He changes us so thoroughly. And that October when I did see her for the last time, she wanted to get up when I left to drive home at 5:30 a.m. She held my hand and said, "Nicki, I love you. You have been the greatest joy of my life." I stood there a bit stunned, and tears ran down my face as I drove away, down our long driveway.

Moma accepted God's love for her. She understood that she would see Jesus face to face, and she read her Bible until her very last day on this earth. God knows her inward parts. He knows yours too, and wants you to follow Him in order to share His love to all around you.

"God wants us to walk in obedience -
not victory. Obedience is oriented toward God;
victory is oriented toward self."

- Jerry Bridges

CHAPTER SEVEN

My Responsibility

"Commit your works to the LORD
And your plans will be established."
PROVERBS 16:3

Midway through my college years, I started to really appreciate friends giving me suggestions for books to read. I had been a Christian for about eight years, and looked for ways to learn and grow. A popular author in the 80's and 90's was Anne Ortlund - someone gave me her best seller at the time, "Disciplines of the Beautiful Woman."

It was a short book and an easy read. Wow. She fit a lot of instructions into that little book. A lot of wisdom, I should say. I decided I would read the book once a year. I did that for a few years, but also read other books, and had many of her "disciplines" planted in my mind. Her suggestions were practical things we should do to free up our time and energy to be able to help someone else, do something productive, or anything besides constantly reorganizing. I admit that I am not the best at this. If I feel overwhelmed with a mess, sometimes I do not know where to start. But maybe the reason this book was so helpful to me was because it gave concrete ways to live a practical and godly life. One thing that stuck out to me was that the passage in Proverbs 31, about being a virtuous woman, has 23 verses on the subject so she said she gave about a 23rd of her day to make up and hair, since there is only one verse about it. Another idea is that if you have an organized purse, then if you need to switch to another purse real quick for some reason, it's super fast. These may seem trivial, but the point is to redeem our time. I think we over plan our days now. We are so busy that we often forget that we are to serve God and others. Anne Ortlund wrote other books too. My favorite is, "Fix Your Eyes On Jesus." I love that book. I have often quoted it in my books or while speaking.

The passage we hear most frequently on spending our time wisely is found in Ephesians 5:16. Paul is telling the believers at Ephesus to walk wisely, and what we do is exposed to the light. God sees all we do. Verses 15-21 tell us,

> *"Therefore be careful how you walk, not as unwise men but as wise, making the most of your time because the days are evil. So then do not be foolish, but understand what the will of the Lord is. And do not get drunk with wine, for that is dissipation, but be filled with the Spirit, speaking to one another in psalms and hymns and spiritual songs, singing and making melody with your heart to the Lord; always giving thanks for all things in the name of our Lord Jesus Christ to God, even the Father; and be subject to one another in the fear of Christ."*

So how DO I spend my time? What IS my responsibility? I admit I do not always fill my time with important things. I sometimes spend hours doing unnecessary things. Does this verse mean we shouldn't have fun or spend time with family? I don't think so. I think it is referring more to useless things overtaking our time. Things like social media, hours scrolling, and television, which started it all.

Please do not misunderstand me, I watch TV too, but I have to admit that I think TV has stolen an entire way of living. Big statement I know. It is so easy to just sit down on a free evening, and automatically turn on the TV. Have you ever thought about what people did after dinner before they had TV? I do not have an answer for what could help us with this, but I just TRY to not make TV time a focus. It is tough though. I am glad my kids are grown and I do not have to be concerned about "screen time" the way parents now are but adults have a distraction problem, too.

I have a phone, and I am on it too much, I am sure. I think we just need to be aware of these things. Set goals. Be outside, accomplish tasks, get to know your neighbors, spend time interacting with your family, and make sure that these things are just as important to you as isolating yourself in front of a screen.

I remember hearing that Charles Wesley, the great theologian and preacher of the reformation, had said that the more he knew God the more time he spent in prayer and saw how much more he needed God. He would stay up until 3 in the morning praying. We use so many excuses about how busy we are, and how we do not have enough time to serve. Those are just excuses. I am guilty of this. I am easily pulled aside by a million things to do. But as you pray in the morning, communicate that to God. Ask Him to help you stay focused each day.

As a younger person I read my Bible sporadically for a while, and I admit I have done that in several stages of life. I get into studying then something pulls my time away. I think of my Moma later in life studying her Bible over and over. That did not come easy. After my grandpa died, and us kids were away living life, and growing up, Moma was all alone in our dreary house on the farm. Our church had gone through a split so she quit going, and not a whole lot of people checked on her. I'm not sure how her relationships with friends were but I'm sure she felt lonely or angry or isolated at times.

She had little funds, and I cannot imagine how hard it was for her to just sit alone at home for years. And years. She began changing. And strength that only God can provide filled her. She transferred her negativity to positivity, and began praying. A few years later my sister, brother-in-law, and I went home. That's when Sam and Lisa decided they would move to the farm to be near Moma. Moma started going to a little church with them, and met friends who she prayed for and started calling each day. Life changed. She still had vestiges of times gone by, but the last 25 years of her life were her happiest. She was the greatest example of a life completely changed by God!

Moma died at 97. I sang, "His Eye is on the Sparrow" at her funeral because God faithfully took care of her for years. And if you know the song the final phrase is, *"His eye is on the sparrow, and I know He watches me."*

I think of the dozens of people she helped and prayed for. It is amazing. So praying and ministering to others is something we can fill our time with, and is a way we can show God's powerful love to others. Sharing your own story of what God has done in your life can greatly encourage someone else, and you can also ask them what God has done for them.

Only by studying His Word can we fully know God. Over the years, I started reading the Word more regularly, and studying my favorite books in the Bible. Really studying, praying scripture, and memorizing it. But I have to say, about 10 years ago I decided to do the "read the Bible in 90 days" thing. It took me more like 230 days. But that was still ok. The point is not to take away from studying in depth, but by reading it quickly through, one gets a different overview. Sort of like reading a novel. All the pieces all fit together like a puzzle. I enjoyed it so much and highly recommend it.

My friend, Mike, also has read the entire Bible. He shares about growth in his life, and how God has continually directed him to His Word.

I have attended the same church since age 3, and I was saved at the age of 7. I was saved because of the fear of God's wrath and Hell.

I was Baptized at the age of 10 and rededicated my life to Christ at Church Camp at age of 13. I have serious dyslexia, and I could barely read and write in my youth. Because of that I didn't read the Bible. In school I was always placed in remedial classes but still did poorly and struggled.

I always thought that good Christian kids did really well in school, and I didn't. I was living a double life, a Christian life on the weekends, and a rowdy life during the week. I didn't really fit in anywhere and didn't have many friends, so I hung out with kids that were not a good influence on me.

I had a reputation of being a bit of a rebel, and I was always getting in trouble. I struggled with this till I was a Junior in High School.

Then, I met a girl at church that I felt was a good Christian girl, unlike the other girls I was hanging out with at the time, and I was ready for a change. Our church got a youth Pastor about 1974 who led the youth group in Bible studies, and made me far more accountable than I had been.

In Senior year, I approached everything differently. I still struggled horribly with academics because of my dyslexia, but I was trying to focus on being a Christian.

Everyone at school that knew me really didn't accept it, so that forced me to be an introvert at school. I lost some friends that I needed to lose. My time was spent with my girlfriend and friends at church.

After getting married and having my first child, I revisited my youth Pastor, and he challenged me in my knowledge of the Bible, and I was convicted because it was true. That's when I realized that it was time for me to start reading and studying the Bible, and I read it through for the first time in my life.

Since that time, I have read the entire Bible several times, and the New Testament over a dozen times. I thoroughly enjoy reading and studying God's word on a daily basis at this point in my life. God has truly blessed me in so many ways, and I am forever grateful that I have Christ in my life.

Mike

The steadying force in Mike's life was to spend time in God's Word. That is true for me, too. It has helped me understand who God is: that He is holy, and righteous, and a judge. The Bible is our guidebook that instructs us in our walk with Him, and it is our responsibility to know and understand it. I've found that consistency helps to create an intentional daily routine of putting God first.

What is our responsibility as believers in Christ? What is first in our life? What encompasses our life? God? Family? Work? God warns us throughout scripture to keep our eyes on Him, and pay attention to what He shows us. We are to spend our time wisely, and seek to do what God has for us. Examine what you spend time doing - are there changes God would have you make?

What would God have us do? John 14:15 gives us a simple but powerful answer,

"If you love Me, you will keep My commandments."

Obeying God is the manifestation of our love for Him. We may not always know how to do that, but we can always pray for direction and He will answer. Second John 1:6 tells us,

> *"And this is love, that we walk in obedience to His commands. As you have heard from the beginning, His command is that you walk in love." (NIV)*

Loving God and others, and obeying Him is our responsibility. As we grow in our faith, we will love others more and will desire to follow God's direction. We pray for Him to show us ways to serve and what path to follow. The journey is long, and the path may grow steep and rocky, but we keep moving forward as He leads us.

"But God has not called us to be like those around us. He has called us to be like Himself. Holiness is nothing less than conformity to the character of God."

- Jerry Bridges

CHAPTER EIGHT

Be Holy As I Am Holy

"As obedient children, do not be conformed to the former lusts which were yours in your ignorance but like the Holy One who called you, be holy yourselves also in all your behavior because it is written, 'YOU SHALL BE HOLY, FOR I AM HOLY'."

1 PETER 1:14-16

We hear so often about being holy. What does that mean exactly?

There are some crazy definitions for this, but the one that describes what we see in the Bible is, "a state of being set apart, consecrated, and dedicated to God." We consider a holy person to be dedicated to God, reverent, with spiritual purity and moral excellence. We are called to be like Christ, set apart. We are to pursue holiness. The Bible tells us in 1 Samuel 2:2,

> *"There is no one holy like the LORD. Indeed, there is no one besides You,*
>
> *Nor is there any rock like our God."*

We are not God. Over and over and over in the Old Testament, it talks about God's holiness. Holiness is the central theme in Leviticus.

> *"Then the LORD spoke to Moses saying, Speak to all the congregation of the sons of Israel and say to them, 'You shall be holy, for I the LORD your God am holy.'" Leviticus 19:1-2*

Why do we need to strive to be holy? Because then others can see God in us. Holy living among God's people. We are to live holy lives. Jerry Bridges' book, *The Pursuit of Holiness,* is well-known. He worked over 60 years with The Navigators, a world-wide Christian organization that shares the gospel and teaches disciple-making. Some key quotes from Jerry Bridges on holiness are: *"No one can attain any degree of holiness without God working in his life, but just as surely, no one will attain it without effort on his own part. God has made it possible for us to walk in holiness. But he has given to us the responsibility of doing the walking; He does not do that for us."*[5] and *"The pursuit of holiness requires sustained and vigorous effort."*[6]

God has called us to a holy calling.

> *"Who saved us and called us to a holy calling, not because of our works but because of his own purpose and grace, which he gave us in Christ Jesus before the ages began." 2 Timothy 1:9 (ESV)*

God calls us much like He did Isaiah. "Holy, Holy, Holy is the LORD of Hosts! The whole earth is full of His glory." Isaiah heard God and recognized his sinfulness, but he knew God called him and responded, "Here I am, send me!" What is our response? If he called

---

5 Jerry Bridges, *The Pursuit of Holiness,* (Colorado Springs,CO: NavPress, 2006), xi-xii.

6 Jerry Bridges, *The Discipline of Grace* (Colorado Springs, CO: NavPress, 2006), 2.

us, we should be obedient and follow Christ, striving to be like Him. It is the call of the elect. We are justified when we accept Christ, sanctified as we grow to be like Him, and then glorified.

There are probably not a lot of Bible passages that are more appropriate for a book on sanctification than the passage in chapter 15 of the Gospel of John. The vine and the branches. This metaphor is used because people of that century lived an agrarian life. God the Father is the vinedresser who takes care of the vine. The vine is Jesus. The vine has two types of branches: those who bear fruit and those who do not bear fruit. God tends the vine and will remove branches that do not bear fruit. In verse 2, it tells us that God prunes. He removes things in a believer's life that may hinder growth, just as a farmer cuts away parts that may not allow the plant to grow productively.

> *"I am the true vine, and My Father is the vinedresser. Every branch in Me that does not bear fruit, He takes away; and every branch that bears fruit, He prunes it so that it may bear more fruit. You are already clean because of the word which I have spoken to you. Remain in Me, and I in you. Just as the branch cannot bear fruit of itself but must remain in the vine, so neither can you unless you remain in Me. I am the vine, you are the branches; the one who remains in Me, and I in him bears much fruit, for apart from Me you can do nothing. If anyone does not remain in Me, he is thrown away like a branch and dries up; and they gather them and throw them into the fire, and they are burned. If you remain in Me, and My words remain in you, ask whatever you wish, and it will be done for you. My Father is glorified by this, that you bear much fruit, and so prove to be My disciples. Just as the Father has loved Me, I also have loved you; remain in My love. If you keep My commandments, you will remain in My love; just as I have kept My Father's commandments and remain in His love. These things I have spoken to you so that My joy may be in you, and that your joy may be made full." John 15:1-11*

Those who "abide" or "remain" in Him, those who bear fruit, submit to God. They are devoted to God and what He has for them. In verse 11 it says, "that your joy may be full." Jesus wants believers to have joy if they walk as God instructs them.

I want that kind of joy, don't you? There is a peace within you when you know you are in God's will. When you have sin blocking your relationship with God, you do not feel connected to Him. A wall grows between us and God, and then we cannot even talk to Him. We feel dread. We must confess sin daily to keep that path clear in order to abide in Him. He has called us to be holy - set apart from sin, set apart to God. Not sometimes, but all the time.

He can and will transform believers into His image. As a teen I went to a Christian camp for high schoolers. On the summer gospel team that led music was Jim. Jim always had a smile on his face. When I went to college, at the same college the team was from, he had already graduated but was still in the area and had married my friend's sister. I did not know Jim well, but admired his love for God that was evident to those around him. He describes his struggle in his journey to becoming more Christlike.

"Such a large crowd of witnesses is all around us! So we must get rid of everything that slows us down, especially the sin that just won't let go. And we must be determined to run the race that is ahead of us." Hebrews 12:1 (CEV)

Some people struggling with an issue in their life find, at some point, clear and complete deliverance from the sin that is destroying them. I consider them to be blessed. I cannot say the same for myself. From an early age I have battled the greatest battle one can ever do warfare with . . . that of self, selfishness, and pride. It is a battle that goes everywhere I go, and I am reminded constantly of my humanity and weakness. I once had a close advisor friend say to me: "Jim, it's for the rest of your life!" Wiser, more revealing words, I have never heard!

In warfare, in battles, there are injuries, deep wounds. Some heal, some are slow, some just fester and require surgery. All leave scars in this lifetime. They remind, they scold, they accuse, and breed fear. This is NOT a battle of man to man! It is not one where excuses work! It is NOT about someone of the past, or circumstances that one can blame, wringing their hands and saying, "It is not my fault!" I am responsible to God for me and me only! People and circumstances are only the tool of revealing to me the real me, and the issues that I must face in my life. It is not about comparative thinking. God wants me, and deals with me, according to who I am and what He desires me to become. He uses people and circumstances, but they are not the cause or the problem. God says to me, "Jim, I will deal with them, what I need from you is you, not them. Paul in Philippians 1:6 says,

"being confident of this very thing, that He who has begun a good work in you will complete it until the day of Jesus Christ." (NKJ)

I love the passage of Hebrews 12:4-7a, and 12-13 (ESV):

"In your struggle against sin you have not yet resisted to the point of shedding your blood. And have you forgotten the exhortation that addresses you as sons? 'My son, do not regard lightly the discipline of the Lord, nor be weary when reproved by Him. For the Lord disciplines the one He loves, and chastised every son whom He receives. It is for discipline that you have to endure. God is treating you as sons.' . . . Therefore lift your drooping hands and strengthen your weak knees, and make straight paths for your

feet, so that what is lame may not be put out of joint but rather be healed."

I love this because it gives me hope, seeing that the disciplining hand of my LORD is actually a real and vivid sign of His love for me and that I indeed belong to Him as His child.

I wish I could say that it has been easy or that victory has been clear and complete, but that would be a lie. I wish I could say that I have lived happily ever after. The day of Christ is coming! It is His to determine when and how I am to arrive at that point. I am content in that realization! In the meantime the battle rages, the warfare continues. James 1: 2-4 says,

"My brethren count it all joy when you fall into various trials (temptations, testings), knowing that the testing of your faith produces patience. But let patience have its perfect work, that you may be perfect and complete, lacking nothing." (NKJ)

Sometimes I dread the illustration used in Hebrews 12:15-17 of Esau:

"See to it that no one fails to obtain the grace of God; <u>that no 'root of bitterness</u>' springs up and causes trouble, and by it many become defiled; that no one is sexually immoral or unholy like Esau, who sold his birthright for a single meal. For you know that afterward, when he desired to inherit the blessing, he was rejected, for he found no chance to repent, though he sought it with tears." (ESV)

At times I too weep finding no seeming rescue from my struggles of self. Yet, Father God's Spirit, Holy Spirit, comes along side and bears witness with my spirit that I am His child and nothing, or anyone can take that away from me!

I am looking unto Jesus and to the things above as my ONLY hope and I find rest in Him as I live in the trenches of this life. Therein I find His joy that carries me along. Though I am battered, wounded, and troubles seem to come from every direction, and for a moment I can't even see out of the foxhole I am in, still I will trust in Him, for He cares for me, I AM HIS CHILD!

Jim

Jim's testimony tugged at my heart. I totally understand some of his struggles and concerns. It definitely spoke to me. And looking above is the key. As believers we have the Holy Spirit in us. The Spirit works in us and helps us on our journey to holiness.

"Lord, give me firmness without hardness,
steadfastness without dogmatism,
love without weakness."

- Jim Elliot

CHAPTER NINE

Steadfast

"With all my heart I have sought You;
do not let me wander from Your commandments!"
PSALM 119:10

When I was in college, there was a woman who ran the college bookstore, lovingly referred to as "Mrs. C." She was tall, with auburn hair, and huge soulful eyes. Students could walk into the little store and she immediately sensed how their day had gone. Had they done poorly on an exam? Were they having problems with a friend, or even a boyfriend or girlfriend? College kids are full of emotion and life struggles. She had a great laugh, and was also full of compassion. The bookstore at that time was in a little stone building on lower campus where many students would pass from the dorms to classes. Easy to stop in, but I do believe kids just stopped in because they sought some wisdom from a listening heart.

Fast forward a few decades, and I heard from her. I learned someone had written a book entitled, "Lunches with Loretta": a book about Mrs. C. - Loretta Chalfant. She had been living for many years in Northern California, I heard, so I bought this amazing book, and loved it so very much. I will read it over again and again, I am sure. The first thing that struck me about this book was near the beginning. The author of the book attended Loretta's church and one day Loretta called her, and asked her if she might like to meet with her on occasion. The author, Karen Foster, said an adrenaline rush went through her, and she wondered why Loretta would want to meet with her - a deacon's wife, who was mature in her faith. But she loved and respected Loretta, and she said yes to meeting with her. Whenever Loretta talked with her at church, Loretta always looked at Karen and really listened. Whenever Loretta spoke at women's Bible study, Karen noticed that *"flecks of golden light danced in her teary brown eyes. Her words were brief but rang of someone who'd sat at God's feet and knew him in a personal way that filled me with awe."*[7]

The entire way to meet with her at lunch, Karen questioned herself. Did Loretta see something wrong in me? She was concerned - What did Loretta want to talk to her about? But they had a great lunch full of sweet conversation, and then Loretta said, *"I want to challenge you to ask God to teach you his lessons no matter the cost."* [8]Their conversation went back and forth.

Then Karen asked, *"Loretta, I know God uses our circumstances to teach us. He doesn't need our permission. So what's the point in asking God to teach us?" Loretta responded, 'You're right. At the end of the day, we really don't have any control about our lessons we're taught. But I believe saying that prayer shows God we're willing to surrender control and step out of our comfort zone to learn His lessons... I also believe that prayer affects how we view our circumstances. Because then, even*

---

7 Karen Foster, *Lunches with Loretta* (United States: Karen Foster, 2020), 5.

8 Karen Foster, *Lunches with Loretta* (United States: Karen Foster, 2020), 11.

our worst-case scenarios are seen as an opportunity for God's Spirit to teach us and make us more like Christ."[9]

I could quote from this entire book. Each page is amazing. Being mentored by a godly person is a critical way we can grow in our walk with God, and be encouraged to become steadfast.

The definition of steadfast is - resolutely or dutifully firm and unwavering. Spiritually it also means being firm in our faith, not letting adversity sway us. So how do we get there? How do we glorify God in all we do, no matter what happens? Christian maturity takes time and grit. Spending time with God in prayer and the Word, spending time with Godly believers, and hearing the truth spoken to us. We need all these components in our life.

As I was thinking about the word "steadfast," I thought about so many people in the Bible who were immovable in their faith, like Daniel. As a young man, he refused to eat meat offered to idols, and requested a different diet. When older, and a high government official, at the peril of his own life, Daniel continued to pray to God in full view of everyone, even though he was commanded not to. He did not care that he might be thrown into prison or worse. He stood firm, immovable, steadfast. Because God was his all in all, he was not going to go against his belief and God's commands, no matter the consequences.

There are so many others in the Bible who also stood firm. Let's take a look at Job: a man who had lost his wealth, his family and his health due to no fault of his own. Chapter 23 reveals Job's character and commitment to God.

> *Then Job replied, even today my complaint is rebellion; His hand is heavy despite my groaning. Oh that I knew where I might find Him, that I might come to His seat! I would present my case before*

9 Karen Foster, *Lunches with Loretta (*United States: Karen Foster, 2020), 11.

Him and fill my mouth with arguments. I would learn the words which He would answer, and perceive what He would say to me.

Would He contend with me by the greatness of His power? No, surely He would pay attention to me. There the upright would reason with Him; and I would be delivered forever from my Judge. Behold I go forward but He is not there, and backward but I cannot perceive Him, when He acts on the left I cannot behold Him; He turns on the right, I cannot see Him.

But He knows the way I take; when He has tried me I shall come forth as gold. My foot has held fast to His path; I have kept His way and not turned aside. I have not departed from the command of His lips; I have treasured the words of His mouth more than my necessary food.

But He is unique and who can turn Him? And what His soul desires, that He does. For He performs what is appointed for me, and many such decrees are with Him.

Therefore, I would be dismayed at His presence; when I consider, I am terrified of Him. It is God who has made my heart faint, and the Almighty who has dismayed me. But I am not silenced by the darkness, nor deep gloom which covers me."

Even though Job couldn't always sense God's presence, he was committed to obedience. He knew God was all powerful and in control over Job's life.

Although there are so many other Bible examples of standing firm and being immovable, there are also many historical and contemporary believers who have weathered the tests of life and chosen to be steadfast. Missionaries are such a great example to us all. They sacrificially give their time, working with limited resources and frequently without any praise. People like Amy Carmichael, an Irish missionary in the early 1900s, who chose to stay in India her entire adult life to help young children who were given to the Hindu priests to be temple prostitutes. She opened and operated an orphanage, and is reported to have saved over 1,000 children during her lifetime.

I think of another great servant like Elisabeth Elliot. She ministered to the very people who killed her husband because she knew God had called her to share God's love and salvation with them.

Or Joni Eareckson Tada, a quadriplegic woman, who has ministered to thousands, sharing hope through suffering to the special needs community. I could list hundreds more who serve or have served God and have stood firm through extremely difficult circumstances. Their lives may be difficult, but their love for God and their trust in His path for them far outweighs any trial.

God wants us to be steadfast, immovable. What stands in the way? I have often felt that the more things I don't share with Him, the more a brick wall is built. Soon I feel unworthy to talk with Him. But He is waiting. Waiting for us to share our hearts. Then when we finally talk to Him, this sense of calm washes over us. Peace. It is a wonderful thing, dear reader. For me, getting outdoors fills me. It allows me to think and pray. When we are filled with Him, then we can be truly steadfast, unwavering, and serving Him. We all need a place or time that helps us to understand what God wants for us. A steady devotion time or prayer time establishes a more intimate relationship with our creator. It helps us to remain consistent and solid. Do you have a special place to read His Word and pray?

I've learned a lot from my time in God's Word, but I have always particularly loved the Psalms because they speak to me in a way other books in the Bible don't. And I have often thought about how David yells at God and is so very honest with Him. Brutally honest. Even when he has sinned, David tells God, and then always gives Him glory and praise. He loves God so very much. I think that is one reason he is called a "man after God's own heart."

Wouldn't you like to be a man or woman after God's own heart? Like David or Loretta? I know I do.

But I can think of many times when I just did what I wanted, and deep down knew it was wrong. Oh how we grieve the Spirit. Sometimes we are stubborn and may "think" we know best, or maybe we waver because instead of holding true we are just wanting to do our own thing. We may block Him out. Thankfully, God overrules our plans sometimes.

"The mind of man plans his way, but the Lord directs his steps." Proverbs 16:9

He is sovereign and in control. We are not. Thank goodness. So what is it that holds us steady? It is when we allow God to be in control.

"So this I say, and affirm together with the Lord, that you walk no longer just as the Gentiles also walk, in the futility of their mind, being darkened in their understanding, excluded from the life of God because of the ignorance that is in them, because of the harness of their heart; and they, having become callous, have given themselves over to sensuality for the practice of every kind of impurity with greediness. But you did not learn Christ in this way, if indeed you have heard Him, and have been taught in Him, just as truth is in Jesus, that in reference to your former manner of life, you lay aside the old self, which is being corrupted in accordance with the lusts of deceit, and that you be renewed in the spirit of your mind, and put on the new self, which in the likeness of God has been created in righteousness and holiness of the truth." Ephesians 4:17-24

We should not walk as unbelievers. Unbelievers are separated from God but we have the Spirit. If we are renewed from our sinfulness at salvation, God will help us in hard situations. We take off our old filthy clothes and are made new.

When we hear of steadfastness we often hear, "remain steadfast". Why is that? We are encouraged to stay steady and headed in the right direction. We have a complete moral compass that directs our steps - the Holy Spirit. We need to pursue righteousness and work for the kingdom. I reiterate: praying each day for God to give us guidance, confess sin, stay in the Word, and not neglecting to attend church all help us to keep on the right track.

It has always been hard for me to be consistent. My mind jumps around and ideas are rampant. It is work for me to stay the course. Sometimes I look at how different we all are, and think about my faults and my dear friends who seem like they have their acts together. But then I realize He made me this way for His purposes, and we all struggle in different ways. We are pieces to an enormous puzzle in the body of Christ. We do have the same rule book, and the same Lord and Savior. Remaining steadfast and following Him are still my instructions.

> *"Do all things without grumbling and disputing, that you may be blameless and innocent, children of God without blemish in the midst of a crooked and twisted generation, among whom you shine as lights in the world, holding fast to the word of life." Philippians 2:14-16a (ESV)*

We must shine God's character to the world. Knowing God's Word helps us to be steadfast because we know Him. When we complain about life, we are directing our complaints against God. So dear one, remain steadfast, do not waver in what He has for you. Understand that He has a perfect plan for you, and He will be with you every step of the way.

"God will ensure my success is in accordance with His plan, not mine."

- Francis Chan

CHAPTER TEN

Trust The Plan

"Though the fig tree should not blossom
and there be no fruit on the vines,
though the yield of the olive should fail
and the fields produce no food,
though the flock should be cut off from the fold,
and there be no cattle in the stalls,
Yet I will exult in the LORD,
I will rejoice in the God of my salvation.
The LORD GOD is my strength,
and He has made my feet like hinds' feet,
And makes me walk on my high places.
For the choir director, on my stringed instruments.
HABAKKUK 3:17-19

A couple years after college, I met Craig, who I would end up marrying. We both worked at a local amusement park. I went to a matinee with him one afternoon with my apartment roommate, and came home to a group of friends who had showed up to have a time of worship and Bible study, something this group did randomly and often. I asked Craig what he wanted to do, and he decided to stay. After some praise songs and prayers, Craig needed to go so he could get up early for work. I walked him out to his car, and he turned to me and said, "I have never been to anything like that before. I got saved at a junior high youth retreat, but then came home to my church that doesn't study the Bible."

A green light went off in my head. All I heard was that he was a believer. Hey, I could date this guy! And so it began.

The next couple years were some tough years. We had many issues to work through. Neither of us were truly living for God, and I see now that God loved me so much that He had to give me consequences. Through that time I ended up starting my first prayer journal and cried out to Him. I read Psalms over and over. I loved that God loved David even after he sinned, and still used him for His purposes. Craig proposed, and of course I went to my favorite professor to ask him to perform the wedding. He questioned me, in front of shy 20 year old Craig: "Why are you marrying him?" I was shocked he would ask that question in front of Craig. Here was a man who had taught several of my Bible classes, joked with me during class "show me your faith by your works," and gave me a job. I had been surrounded by mature Godly men, and now I was marrying a new believer. He clearly thought it unwise of me. But, I was a young person, and did not really consider the possible issues this might cause. So, we were married about 6 months later. We moved to the coast of Central California where Craig was finishing his degree in computer science. We had a great church there, with friends we still hold dear. Craig worked and went to school, and I was pregnant with our daughter Jessica. He graduated, and we moved to the Bay Area where all good software engineers go.

Life was busy, and we got involved in our church, but wanted out of California. We made great friends there, who are still our friends. I will be forever grateful for our young married life with faithful friends around us, and also for the fact Craig always wanted us to be at church, even though he was still new in his faith. Then Craig transferred with his company to Idaho. I had never been to Idaho before the first interview he had there. The pastor and wife, who had been at my little church in Washington when my dad died, were serving there in Idaho. We visited their church, and I knew some of the people there from college. So great! I admit I was wanting Craig to take a bigger role in leading our family spiritually. He was so faithful in having us always going to church, but I wanted more. Bottom line, I was discontent. By then, I had 4 kids under the age of 6, plus a puppy. I had let frustration and discontent move into my life.

Then, our oldest, Jessica, became thirsty all the time, and had some other problems too. I told the pediatrician, and he said to make a chart, marking down every time she drank and every time she used the restroom. It was a lot. He had said we did not need an appointment, but to just come in and do a quick urine test. So the next afternoon, I got a neighbor to watch the other kids, and I took Jessica to the doctor. She did the test, and a few minutes later he came into the waiting room, and said, "Go to the hospital and have a blood test done, then return here at 6:30 with Craig." So I went to the hospital, and when the receptionist asked why I needed a test, I couldn't respond. Jessica was watching me like a hawk, and I squeaked out, "She has too much sugar in her urine." The receptionist quietly took her into the back. We went back that evening, and our doctor explained everything. Then we went to our pharmacist, who gave us all sorts of things I had never used before. I went home, and went down the street to my neighbor who was a Type 1 diabetic, and she showed me how to do a blood test and give a shot.

As we got ready for bed that night, Craig said, "Our life has changed forever." It was so very true. We had no idea what to do or how this would change our life, but the next morning we held down our 6 year old who was screaming as we tried to do a blood test and give her a shot of insulin. I read a lot of information that day, and felt how unfair Type 1 diabetes is. Ninety percent of diabetics are Type 2, many times a result of lifestyle choices. Then there are the children born with a faulty pancreas (Type 1), totally out of their control. I was so heartbroken and stunned by it all. . Why would this happen to our precious little girl? Why had God allowed this to happen? Hadn't we loved Him? What would He teach us through this? It has been over thirty years, and I still cry about this. As I am typing this in a coffee shop, there are tears rolling down my cheeks. BUT, although we may grieve the circumstances, we rejoice in God, for He is faithful. Jessica is a thriving young woman who has overcome great things in life. God is using her and has been carrying out His plan in her life. She works in multiple ministries, and while she has many physical issues due to decades of this disease, she never complains. Her trial has given us all insight and empathy into those who struggle with it.

We have a young couple new to our church that we have gotten to know recently. They are such a joy to us. John has just recently found out that he is a late diagnosed Type 1 diabetic. It squeezes my heart whenever I hear someone newly diagnosed. It is such an adjustment. He shares:

> *I will never forget the disheartening realization that I was, and forever will be, a type 1 diabetic. I remember vividly sitting in that hospital bed, being told the news, my wife sitting in the chair next to me, feeling shattered and broken. I was 25. I made the mistake of looking online at what the average life expectancy of a type 1 was, and I broke down in tears.*
>
> *Three years later, and I still struggle. It's a day-in, day-out ordeal, and some days it feels like I'm on top of the world, while other days feel like a sword to the gut. I wish often that I had never become a diabetic.*

Through it all, I know God is there for me.

I can't explain why it was part of His plan for me to be diabetic. To this day, I wonder in confusion as to what the purpose of it is, or what he could possibly have in store for me that would require such a diagnosis. But I've learned so much these last few years about God, his sovereignty, and our need to trust in Him, and that has helped remind me that there's a purpose for it. Even if I never learn what that purpose is, I know it's necessary to have happened, and necessary for a better future, whether it's my own, for someone else's, or even for the greater good.

I deal with anxiety on a daily basis, often due to my health, but often elsewhere as well. I have to remind myself constantly, "Do not be anxious about anything, but in everything by prayer and pleading with thanksgiving let your requests be made known to God. And the peace of God, which surpasses all comprehension, will guard your hearts and minds in Christ Jesus" (Philippians 4:6-7). He is the one true God who guards us and protects us, who loves us immensely, and who wants us to thrive! He doesn't want us to suffer, but rather strengthen us and rely on Him for all things. I know that He is at my side, even when I'm struggling to keep my blood sugar levels in a healthy range, or whenever I get scared that I'll pass out if I don't eat sugar as soon as possible. I know He is there to protect me.

I may not know why this happened to me, or to anyone else in the world with type 1 diabetes. However, I have peace knowing He has a plan for me. For you. For all of us! And that alone helps me feel like I am capable of anything!

John

John is still grieving his new diagnosis. It takes time to adjust to a new thing in life. We may not always be able to see the good that God has planned. I admit there have been dozens of times in my life that I felt completely overwhelmed by life. But I had to trust His plan. What choice did I have? I have also thought about unbelievers who do not have God to believe in or give them hope. How do they cope with their trials? Sometimes, after I see "the why" something may have happened, then I feel totally blessed - but what if He chooses not to show us? Do we still trust? Proverbs 3:5-6 tells us,

> *Trust in the LORD with all your heart and do not lean on your own understanding. In all your ways acknowledge Him, and He will make your paths straight."*

This is probably a memory verse for many, but I hope that doesn't mean we pay less attention to it. Tell the Lord everything, beloved, He promises to show us the path. Trusting Him deepens our faith.

> *"The LORD is my strength and my shield; my heart trusts in Him, and I am helped; Therefore my heart exults, and with my song I shall thank Him." Psalm 28:7*

> *"Delight yourself in the LORD; and He will give you the desires of your heart. commit your way to the LORD, trust also in Him, and He will do it." Psalm 37:4-5*

So how does God give us the desires of our heart if He is giving us trials? We need to TRUST the plan. So very hard. Maybe your child died or you were just diagnosed with cancer. Maybe you see terrible things happening in the world, and evil people prospering. Sometimes it does not seem fair. When a child, people often say, "That's not fair!" and sometimes the parent will say, "Life is not fair." Very true.

I think that I have had times in my own life that I "thought" something was the desire of my heart, but low and behold, God, in His great mercy saved me from it, and replaced that desire with something far better. His plan – much better than mine.

> *"And God is able to make all grace abound to you, so that having all sufficiency in all things at all times, you may abound in every good work." 2 Corinthians 9:8*

> *"The young lions suffer want and hunger; but those that seek the LORD lack no good thing." Psalm 34:10*

> *"Therefore I tell you, do not be anxious about your life, what you will eat or what you will drink, nor about your body, what you will put on, is not life more than food, and the body more than clothing?" Isaiah 58:11*

Trust God with your whole heart and life. Believe how much He loves you, accept it, and see how He works as you are obedient to Him.

"Christian contentment is that sweet, inward, quiet, gracious frame of spirit, which freely submits to and delights in God's wise and fatherly disposal in every condition."

- Jeremiah Burroughs

CHAPTER ELEVEN

Contentment

"But godliness is actually a means of great gain
when accompanied by contentment.
For we have brought nothing into the world,
so we cannot take anything out of it either.
If we have food and covering,
with these we shall be content."
I Timothy 6:6-8

The book of Timothy was written by the Apostle Paul after he had been in prison in Rome the first time. He wanted to revisit several churches he had been to before. Paul had visited Ephesus previously, and had left Timothy there to help the church work out some issues that had arisen. They needed better, qualified leaders, and they were involved with false doctrine. Paul's letter to Timothy guides and gives instruction for the church. In these verses, Paul is connecting contentment with godliness.

Contentment. What does that mean? What makes us content? Or how do we become content? Does that mean that I should be satisfied with what I have and shouldn't look forward to getting new things like buying a house when we move, or a new car when the old one is broken? Not necessarily. But think about this: are you controlled by discontent? I have had so many conversations with friends over the years who wish life was different. Maybe even wished they had not married their spouse. Are you always wishing life was different? Are you always hoping to change your circumstances for "the better"? I admit that I have questioned what was happening in my life at certain moments, and have struggled with being content at times, but that's all part of our journey as humans.

I hope you have a Paul or Timothy in your life to give you clear direction when you fall into discontent. I have had several people who have filled that role for me, although I think I did not always truly listen to them. Many times WE think we know what's best, and so we do not always listen to wise counsel. But we should.

In college I had much required reading, and some books were extra reading. One book I read and underlined everywhere was "The Keys To Spiritual Growth" by John MacArthur. He has a statement about contentment I underlined, but I don't think I really took it to heart at the time. *"Glorify God by contentment. Discontent characterizes the age in which we live. We may be discontent about ourselves and about our circumstances. But who made you the way you are, minus your sins? God. So you ought to be content with yourself. Who put you where you are with all your circumstances, without your sin? God did. You are what you are, whatever you are, wherever you are because God put you there. When you are content you acknowledge God's sovereignty in your life and that gives Him glory. If you are discontent or malcontent your real complaint is against God's wisdom."* [10]

---

10 John MacArthur, *The Keys to Spiritual Growth,* (Old Tappan, NJ: Fleming H. Revell Company, 1976), 47-48.

This explains a lot. We complain all the time when life throws us a curveball, don't we? We become discontent, and I do not think we are really focusing on the truth of what God has given us and has for us.

I love this quote in the book, "Living By The Book": *"Many christians are like poor photographs - overexposed and underdeveloped. They've had plenty of input from the Word of God, but what difference has it made in their lives? Spiritual growth is a commitment to change. And yet, the human heart resists nothing as strongly as it resists change. We will do anything to avoid it."*[11]

This all takes us back to reading the Word, having friends who point us to God, and praying for contentment and peace. A few years ago, I read the book by Laura Story, "When God Doesn't Fix It." I was blown away. Many of you may know the story behind the song by her, "Blessings." And I knew that song far before I read the book. She writes about how blessings can come through difficult situations. I think sometimes that is very true.

Laura's husband, Martin, had a brain tumor after they had only been married a couple years. The doctors did not know if he would survive the surgery but he did, however, he suffered from short term memory loss, which he still has to this day. He did not remember he was married to her. He knew who she was because she was a worship leader and they had gone to college together, but every day he had to look at a note that told him who he was and that he was married. And then after they had children, the note also told him that he had children. This book is filled with her striving to follow what God wants, but every day was such a struggle; she felt broken for years. She explains how she discovers the blessings in life's unexpected turns. When difficult things happen to you, how do you react? Will you be unhappy forever if your situation never changes? Laura Story relied

---

11 Howard G. Hendricks and William D. Hendricks, *Living by the Book* (Chicago: Moody, 1991), 292.

on God and trusted Him to provide a way to deal with their unique situation.

God does not promise that life will not have any problems or trials. But He does promise to be with us and love us, and give us comfort no matter what happens.

If we are in a state of continual discontent, we can become bitter and resentful. I have met with several people who have gone through a difficult time, and plan on making a poor choice. I have asked them, "What do you think God wants for you?" and they respond, "I think God wants me happy." Nonsense. There is nowhere in Scripture where it tells us that God wants us happy. He wants us to be obedient, to abide in Him. He wants us filled with joy, filled with peace, at rest.

> *"...Jesus said, 'I praise You, Father, Lord of Heaven and earth, that You have hidden these things from the wise and intelligent and have revealed them to infants. Yes, Father, for this way was well pleasing in Your sight. All things have been handed over to Me by My Father; and no one knows the Son except the Father; nor does anyone know the Father except the Son, and anyone to whom the Son wills to reveal Him. Come to Me, all who are weary and heavy laden, and I will give you rest. Take My yoke upon you and learn from Me, for I am gentle and humble in heart, and YOU WILL FIND REST FOR YOUR SOULS. For My yoke is easy and My burden is light.'" Matthew 11:25-30*

It is often difficult to find rest in our soul if we have our head full of discontent, fear, disappointment, impatience, or unforgiveness. There are also stresses we put on ourselves, filling our lives up with too much busyness. We are so overwhelmed with life, how can we possibly be full of His joy and contentment? How can we be at peace with our head and heart filled with everything but God?

Contentment is the attitude of us accepting what God currently has planned for us. A condition of life in which nothing else is needed because God has supplied what we need at the moment. Paul writes in Philippians 4:11-13:

> *"Not that I speak from want, for I have learned to be content in whatever circumstance I am. I know how to get along with humble means, and I also know how to live in prosperity; in any and every circumstance I have learned the secret of being filled and going hungry, both of having abundance and suffering need. I can do all things through Him who strengthens me."*

This passage is a favorite for many. Paul is saying here that he doesn't really worry about his needs because he knows God is taking care of every need that he has, and he trusts Him for it.

I have a friend at our church who had a great struggle for years. I felt connected to her because we are both artists, and I relate to her in many ways. I prayed for her in her great desire for more children, but I had four children and could not fully understand her pain. My moma had 10 miscarriages before she adopted Lisa and I. I knew this was a hard thing for Moma, but after knowing several women with this difficulty, I started to see how very painful this is for a woman. Andrea is an amazing woman with a servant-heart, and I am so very blessed that she shares her painful story with us.

I've grown the most in my life through the hardest seasons. Not just tough days or busy schedules—but soul-stripping, faith-testing seasons. The kind that leaves you wondering who you are and what you actually believe. The kind that feel like loss, but end up birthing something deeper than you could've imagined.

Motherhood started easily for me. I got pregnant without any trouble, and I truly loved stepping into that role. Our first son was (and is!) my delightful, happy, and easy-going child, who made me feel like I was doing a great job. Looking back, I know I gave myself more credit than I should have. It felt like I was thriving—but I was mostly relying on my own strength. And pride. I didn't see it that way at the time, but I can now.

Then came the pruning.

I didn't expect to struggle with growing our family. As a type-A planner, I had it mapped out: two or three kids, spaced just right. But it didn't happen that way. We spent nearly a decade waiting—navigating infertility, devastating diagnoses, endless appointments, and the monthly cycle of hope followed by heartbreak. I'd like to say I clung to Jesus the whole time, but honestly, I mostly clung to my plan. I kept hoping God would bless what I wanted, instead of surrendering to what He might be doing.

Eventually, something shifted. It wasn't dramatic—just quiet and gradual. I started to let go. I began to see the beauty of the life I already had: our incredible son, our marriage, the slower rhythm that waiting had given us. And while I didn't stop longing, I did start trusting—truly trusting—and that led to a peace and joy I hadn't even realized I was missing.

And then—after nearly eleven years—we found out we were pregnant. Naturally. Without intervention. We laughed. Honestly, how could we not? I thought immediately of Sarah and Abraham and their miracle child. That pregnancy felt like redemption. Like God had tenderly closed a chapter I didn't even realize was still open.

But pruning isn't always a one-time thing.

As we approached the birth of our second son, there were a few complications. He spent the first two weeks of his life in the NICU and came home on oxygen. At the time, we didn't know why. It wasn't until months later that we learned he had a brain abnormality that led to an intellectual disability diagnosis.

He's nine now, and we're still learning what that means. There's no timeline for understanding or "outgrowing" what we face. It's ongoing. And it has completely reshaped my motherhood, my faith, and my understanding of what it means to abide.

This pruning—parenting a child with special needs—is deeper than anything I've known. It's taken every illusion of control and stripped it bare. It's revealed my limitations, and made me daily dependent on the strength of Christ. Not "God, help me do this" but "God, I can't do this unless You carry me." The verse in John 15 that says, "Apart from Me, you can do nothing"? I live that now.

But I can also see the fruit. I'm not the same mom I was in the early days. I'm slower now. Gentler. More compassionate. I see people differently. I notice pain I might've missed before. I don't jump to fix things—I've learned that presence is often the best gift we can offer.

Through it all, I've come to believe this: pruning isn't punishment. It's preparation. The Gardener sees the bigger picture, and He knows where to cut so that something deeper, sweeter, and more lasting can grow.

My story is still being written. The pruning continues. But so does the fruit. And so does the abiding.

Andrea

I appreciate Andrea sharing her heart so very openly and completely.

Sanctification and learning contentment in all situations does take time. It is not an easy process. Sometimes we question God, but that is not the answer. I believe that our contentment grows as we mature in our faith. I know I questioned God through dozens of trials, and David also cried out to God over and over again in Psalms. Not because he didn't think God was listening or would help him, but because he loved God and shared his heart with Him. God wants us to communicate with Him.

Share your heart, dear one, tell Him that you are struggling. He is waiting to listen to your pleas for help. He sees your tears. I have something I have been praying for over and over for years. I literally cry every time I pray about it. It strengthens my heart to talk to God about it. AND I know God knows my heart and He already has an answer.

The real challenge is to strive to be content while He is working in our life during the difficult times.

Suffering plays an important role in our lives. It makes us grow. It strengthens us in our faith, and helps us to trust God with our entire life. And sometimes we can see that His timing is better than our own. It is so easy to think we know the solution or the perfect timing, but it is a wonderful thing to leave it in God's sovereign hands, and have peace and contentment.

"He who does not serve God where he is would not serve God anywhere else."

- Charles Spurgeon

CHAPTER TWELVE

In His Service

"Only fear the LORD, and serve Him in truth with all your heart. For consider what great things He has done for you."

1 SAMUEL 12:24

How do we grow in our desire to serve? Without a heart to do what God wants us to, we won't serve. Our heart needs to match His desires and will for our lives. In Luke 6:46-49, Jesus gives an illustration of a heart that follows God.

> *"Why do you call me 'Lord, Lord' and do not do what I say?" Everyone who comes to Me and hears My words and acts on them, I will show you whom he is like: he is like a man building a house, who dug deep and laid a foundation on the rock; and when a flood occurred, the torrent burst against that house and could not shake it, because it had been well built. But the one who has heard and has not acted accordingly, is like a man who built a house on the ground without any foundation; and the torrent*

burst against it and immediately it collapsed, and the ruin of that house was great."

Genuine faith produces obedience, action. It shows our real character and love for our Lord.

We are to be serving. James 1:21-25 tells us to be doers, not just hearers:

"Therefore, putting aside all filthiness and all that remains of wickedness, in humility receive the Word implanted, which is able to save your souls. But prove yourselves doers of the Word, and not merely hearers who delude themselves. For if anyone is a hearer of the word and not a doer, he is like a man who looks at his natural face in a mirror; for once he has looked at himself and gone away, he has immediately forgotten what kind of person he was. But one who looks intently at the perfect law, the law of liberty, and abides by it, not having become a forgetful hearer but an effectual doer, this man will be blessed in what he does."

James is telling us that our entire person should seek to be doing. If not, then we need to look at why. He could just tell us to "do" and not be a "doer." Being a "doer" is an ongoing way of being, not just having a list of things to check off. Believers are guided by the Spirit who will fill us with the desire to serve God.

I love being involved in serving God. I always have from day one. I get a bit overly enthusiastic at times, but it is a favorite thing of mine. I always knew it was something God wanted for each of us, but after years of thinking about the dozens of ways to serve, I started realizing I may not be able to serve in the ways I thought I would. I think when I was younger, I always thought that I would go into full-time Christian service of some sort. Not exactly sure what, but I knew that must be the plan for me. But life took me on a different path for quite awhile. I still ministered to others in a variety of ways. I taught some Bible studies, took some evangelism classes. Met with others to encourage them in their faith, but when we moved to Idaho I had three littles and one on the way. Shortly after, my pastor's wife told me THAT was my ministry - my family. I felt like quipping back, "of course it is." I considered what she said. Yes, I could teach my kids but I could teach others also, right? I wanted to impact more people than just three little kids! My thirties were a time of wishing life was a bit different, I admit. I remember hearing once at a ladies retreat that people are their most unhappy in their 30's. Why, I thought? Was it because life was not turning out according to plan? Did they think it should have been different? I was happy, but I wanted to do more. We worked at church in the AWANA youth program. I sang on the worship team. I had a lovely home, church, kids, and a hardworking husband. But what was missing? Was I growing spiritually?

I knew God wanted me to use whatever He had blessed me with to share with others. We moved to a home with a very large lot, and decided to install a pool. What fun! The kids would think this was great, and they did. We had many church functions in our backyard. For about ten years, we had our annual church picnic at our home. Dinner with 150 people. Volleyball, swimming, lots of food. It was great fun. We also had a summer activity on Thursdays called, "Little Swimmers." From 11 am to 2 pm, between 20-50 people came and played in the pool. I had rules for safety reasons, and usually had someone in the role of lifeguard.

In Paul's second letter to Timothy he instructs believers to endure and work heartily. Verse 2:12-15,

> *"If we endure, we will also reign with Him. If we deny Him, He also will deny us. If we are faithless, He remains faithful, for He cannot deny Himself. Remind them of these things, and solemnly charge them in the presence of God not to wrangle about words, which is useless and leads to the ruin of the hearers. Be diligent*

to present yourself approved to God as a workman who does not need to be ashamed, accurately handling the word of truth."

Believers prove the genuineness of their faith by their actions. If we are faithful and consistent, it shows our faith is real. We can be zealous. We can share the Word accurately, but we also need to work at what God currently has for us. It took me a while to see that my home and family, which was so very important to me, was also the ministry God had for me at that time.

Meanwhile my kids were growing up. They worked at summer camp during high school and college, and Craig was travelling a lot for work. With the kids almost grown and Craig gone so much, our acre and a half, pool, and large home, was feeling empty. I allowed my melancholy personality to take over. There was an emptiness in my life. But wasn't I serving and loving God? Why were things bothering me?

Romans 5:1-5 tells us that hard things produce endurance. I think sometimes we float along with things going well, then something happens that throws us off. Do we get back on track quickly, or do we wallow in it for a while.

"Therefore, having been justified by faith, we have peace with God through our Lord Jesus Christ, through whom also we have obtained our introduction by faith into this grace in which we stand; and we exult in hope of the glory of God. And not only this, but we also exult in our tribulations, knowing that tribulation brings about perseverance; and perseverance, proven character; and proven character, hope; and hope does not disappoint, because the love of God has been poured out within our hearts through the Holy Spirit who was given to us."

We went through some of the hardest years of our lives with really great children who each were finding their way. With them so close in age, I think I was praying harder, and more than ever. We left our home of many years for a smaller property when the kids were mostly out of the house. It was during this time that my moma died, and I saw a change happening in my life. I became an empty nester. After years of people saying, "someone needs to write your story," I decided to write my first book. I wrote about overcoming adversity. I wanted people to see that God uses our brokenness and difficult circumstances for His purposes. He did it in my life, and He can do it in yours too.

One of my dearest and oldest friends and her husband live in Central California, in the middle of orange groves. Cliff grew up there, and works hard in the community that he has been a part of for so many years. It is a tiny town, as many farming communities are. Cliff describes the changing ways his church has served God in their community.

Sometimes God challenges us to serve Him in ways that are outside the norm.

The church I grew up in was an active place where a lot of ministry took place. It was located in a small rural community, and people came from nearby communities to take part in what God was doing there. After I got out of High School, the neighborhood changed, and the local participation in the church changed. Fewer people came from the immediate area, and the folks from further away were drawn to other places.

I stayed active in the life of the church throughout my growing up years. As I became an adult, I was asked to serve in leadership: first on the Deacon Board, then as an Elder. During that time, the church tried to relocate, but it was eventually blocked from moving. Those who remained were discouraged. After our pastor retired, a young pastor came, and the church was revived for a time.

I and another Elder became close friends, and realized that we had the same desire to serve God, see the neighborhood hear about Jesus, and have His love expressed in tangible ways. We worked with the pastor to try and provide opportunities for that to happen, but there was not a lot of response from our people or the neighborhood. After 10 years, the young pastor relocated and the congregation declined again.

For 15 years, my brother Elder and I worked through some really tough times, but we were encouraged by the fact that God was continuing to keep the doors of the church open, even though the attendance continued to decline. We had one vocational pastor for a very short time, but after he left, I began bringing the weekly Sunday messages, while maintaining a farm and raising my family.

With mostly older members, our congregation continued to decline in numbers. We were increasingly called on to look at wrapping things up and closing the church down. Different people, from within the church to people in our denominational leadership, didn't see any "value" in us continuing to serve God in this location. As my co-Elder and I prayed about it, we felt that God was confirming to us that we needed to continue to trust Him, and serve Him in this place. We prayed that God would provide a path for our church to continue to have a Christian influence in our community. God answered our prayers. Within two years of each other, two Spanish-speaking churches began meeting on our facilities, and still are.

We also helped establish a Boys & Girls Club which is located on part of our church facilities. It has been serving our rural area for over 10 years, helping kids navigate the realities of a strong gang presence, persistent drug abuse, and widespread poverty in our community. Although the Club is not a Christian ministry, it is a place where the attendees often tell their leaders that it is the only place they feel safe. That chokes me up when I think of it…

Other than a Sunday morning Service, our English-speaking congregation had no other activity at the facilities. Then came the Lockdowns…

The Lockdowns created issues that affected everyone, attendance-wise. I posted online video devotionals to help fill the gaps while we were physically separated, and then posted the video-recorded Sunday morning messages once we resumed in-person services. But the most obvious effect of the Lockdowns was that it was made it apparent that our congregation would not remain viable.

I served in the lead leadership and teaching role for over 12 years after the last vocational pastor had left. It was not easy, or clear, how things would happen. I tried to encourage whomever would listen: God often works in different ways than our conventional wisdom dictates.

What we did was in contrast to the modern mindset of "value" being found through numbers of attenders, converts, disciples and participants. We are in a community with great needs, and we served God through a process of transitioning from one kind of ministry to another. Though our members no longer meet together, our church facility still hosts the two Spanish-speaking churches and the Boys & Girls Club. We partnered with God to let Him make things happen on our site that will hopefully carry into the future. It is our ongoing prayer that the ministries, and the Club, will be used by the Lord to help people see Jesus.

Cliff

Through the decades of knowing Cliff and my friend, Re, I have seen them be ever faithful to their church, community and friends. You will not find more faithful servants. Although I am sure times have been discouraging through the past several years, they continue to serve. Service to God often changes, and it is not easy to always understand. It is often through heartbreak, but we remain faithful as Cliff has remained steady in serving for decades. This is a great example to us all.

Growing up, my little church went through a split about 50 years ago. But it hung on for a few years and then an amazing man of God came, and it is a thriving church - now stronger than ever.

I have been a part of a couple ministries that changed and I did not understand why but I can still serve in other ways. I have also know missionaries who are so weary of serving but continue to serve because God has told them to.

> *"Rendering service with a good will as to the Lord and not to man, knowing that whatever good anyone does, this he will receive back from the Lord, whether he is slave or free." Ephesians 6:7-8*

God needs His laborers. Serving Him is not always easy, but we have rich spiritual benefits given to us through hard times: perseverance, proven character, and hope. This is a great promise.He grows us through serving Him, and our reward is great.

"God never issues instructions
He is not prepared to equip us to obey."

- Elisabeth Elliot

CHAPTER THIRTEEN

Equipped

"Each of you should use whatever gift you have received to serve others, as faithful stewards of God's grace in its various forms."
1 PETER 4:10 (NIV)

Serving God is an integral part of our Christian faith. By God's grace He helps us to do this. He gives us strength and ability. Several years ago, I was listening to a missionary speak about sleeping with his gun, because people came to him all through the night, and he never knew if it was someone he needed to help or someone there to harm his family. This is commitment folks. He loved the people in that country so very much, and was willing to live in a dangerous place to share the gospel with those people. We may not all be able to work in a place such as that, but God has equipped us to share with others no matter where He has placed us.

We have all been given spiritual gifts to use to serve God. It is not something we create ourselves, but rather how the body of Christ works - like pieces of a puzzle. Fitting together to serve in different ways, benefiting others within the body of Christ. Colossians 3:23-24 states,

> *"Whatever you do, do your work heartily, as for the Lord rather than for men. Knowing that from the Lord you will receive the reward of the inheritance. It is the Lord whom you serve."*

The larger passage in Colossians speaks of slavery, but the idea is don't just work while the master is watching, because the Lord is always watching. The Lord assures the believer that they will receive compensation in eternity. God does not tell us that it is always easy to serve, but that He gifts us with various traits for His purposes.

I love listening to missionary speakers. They inspire me. They are out in the trenches working tirelessly to serve. We are part of their ministry by financially and prayerfully being committed to assisting them. I have heard missionaries who have been in countries for twenty years with few converts. I would feel discouraged. But God knows the hearts, we do not. We do not know what may happen in that next generation.

You may have heard of Jim and Elisabeth Elliot. They were missionaries in Central America. Jim and four other men were killed by a tribe they were trying to reach with the Gospel. Many people questioned why Elisabeth went back to that country to serve after her husband was so brutally murdered. But she knew God had brought her there, and wanted her to continue to serve. Years later that very village had many come to Christ, and she was able to minister to the very people that had never heard the gospel - people whom her husband had wanted to minister to. Elisabeth eventually returned to the United States to write over 20 books. "Through Gates of Splendor" and "Shadow of the Almighty" are two that are the most well known. I am amazed by her dedication.

As God molds us into who we are to become in Him, we gradually start to trust Him, even when trials happen. We know and understand that He is in control, and has us exactly where we need to be. I have delayed using this very well known verse in Romans, not wanting people to think it is overused or a cliche,' but it is in God's Word and will never be cliche'.

> *"And we know that God causes all things to work together for good to those who love God, to those who are called according to His purpose." Romans 8:28*

God makes all things happen according to HIS purpose. ALL things: hard times, good times, death, life, suffering, temptation. God calls us to salvation and the process begins. For His glory and for our benefit, here and eternity.

Our close friends that we have known for 40 years went through great hardship within their family a few years ago. Life is so very painful sometimes. However, Mark was able to recognize that God had equipped him to weather the storm gracefully and in peace. Mark shares his story with us.

God has blessed us with the sanctification process—a continuous refining of the elect as we walk through life. One of the clearest signs of salvation is the Holy Spirit working within us, shaping our hearts and minds toward Him.

Yet, life is full of challenges, and God never promised His followers an easy path. Nowhere in Scripture does it say that God desires us to simply be "happy." Instead, He calls us to deeper understanding, perseverance, and unwavering faith in His sovereignty. Like a wise coach preparing His players for the game, God strengthens us through trials to ready us for what lies ahead.

It's during the good times that we must seek Him earnestly and wrestle with difficult questions. One question that often weighs on believers is: "How could a good God allow bad things to happen to good people?" Delving into this question is beyond the scope of these few words. Nevertheless, we must acknowledge that we are finite beings trying to comprehend an infinite God. We will never know why He does what He does. We are called to simply trust.

I faced this truth in a deeply personal way when our one-year-old granddaughter was diagnosed with leukemia. Watching her suffer through treatments, painful reactions to medication, and long hospital stays was unbearable. Yet, in the midst of my deepest sorrow, a peace washed over me—a peace that was entirely unnatural, beyond human comprehension. "Peace in pain." was the way I described it then and now.

As the hardship intensified, I didn't find myself asking "Why?" Not because the suffering was easy, but because God had faithfully prepared me. Studying His sovereignty and meditating on His character had given me the foundation to endure. What I had not anticipated, however, was the compounded anguish of watching not only my granddaughter suffer but also my own child walk through the sorrow of a parent's worst nightmare.

And yet, through it all, God was there. He had equipped me, strengthened me, and sustained me. The glory for that preparation belongs to Him alone.

Life will bring difficulties, but in those moments, we can rest in the assurance that He has prepared us for those moments. As believers, may we continue to seek Him in times of peace so that when the storms arrive, our trust in His sovereign plan will remain unwavering.

Mark

Mark has been going through a painful time, but he recognizes that our holy God has equipped him for this season of life.

So how does God equip us? He gives us spiritual fruit in our life.

> *"But the fruit of the Spirit is love, joy, peace, patience, kindness, goodness, faithfulness, gentleness, self-control; against such things there is no law. Now those who belong to Christ Jesus have crucified the flesh with its passions and desires. If we live by the Spirit, let us also walk by the Spirit. Let us not become boastful, challenging one another, envying one another." Galatians 5:22-26*

Godly attitudes characterize a believer's life. That is where the equipping begins. It must. It produces fruit that God uses: love, joy, peace, patience, kindness, goodness, faithfulness, gentleness, and self-control. He has equipped us in ways so that others see Him clearly.

He has also given us gifts.

> *"And He gave some as apostles and some as prophets, and some as evangelists, and some as pastors and teachers, for the equipping of the saints for the work of service, to the building up of the body of Christ, until we all attain to the unity of the faith, and of the knowledge of the Son of God, to a mature man, to the measure of the stature which belongs to the fullness of Christ." Ephesians 4:11-13*

I have taken that assessment to identify our spiritual gifts about six times, at various retreats and classes over maybe a forty year span. I always try to be as honest as possible when answering the questions, because I truly want to know my gifts. No one ever sees the test so what does it matter? No subterfuge. Amazingly, over forty years, my gifts have mostly remained the same. Not a surprise, but one thing I have noticed: a couple of the scores have increased over the years, like evangelism. In the past, I had a bit of a score with it, but it has greatly increased. My gifts are Pastor-teacher, exhortation, prophecy, and evangelism. I really wondered as a younger person how I scored high for pastor/teacher. There are two pastor gifts, one being more administrative (definitely not me), and one more teaching-focused. Then I realized it wasn't about being a pastor, but wanting to teach the Word and care for those in the church body. And why does prophecy always pop up? That puzzled me. Later I learned that prophecy is not foretelling the future, but it is speaking a message from God/His Word for a specific situation or circumstance. As a Bible teacher I take that very seriously. The thing to remember about this is that God gifts all of us. He equips us to be part of a big puzzle that all fits together.

There are so many things that can be grace killers in our life. God gives us tools to equip us, and we can reject the gifts, or allow other things to get in the way. The main thing is sin. I have ignored God's voice in my life many times. Because I was selfish and thought I knew what was best or just did not care, I let petty things like pride, thinking I was right, slander, envy, and jealousy hinder my growth. Sure, I said I loved God, and I knew He loved me, but I followed my own path, not God's. As a believer in Christ, God always showed me my sin. As we grow, we can see it more clearly, and can repent. Daily confession helps to clear away anything blocking our relationship with our holy God.

God also directs our paths. He shows us how we fit perfectly into His plan. We only need to be tuned in to what His plans are.

The Holy Spirit works in us to transform us to become more like Christ. We are on a lifelong journey of growth to become holy. Our hearts change, and we love God and others even more. This is not from a single event but it is a lifelong process. We must choose not to sin and to obey God in what He has for us to do. And so we reflect Christ.

What about you, dear one? Are you praying and looking at how He has equipped you? Has He given you a life you can share with others? Ask Him for direction and He will answer you. Maybe not exactly in how you thought, but in a way that will be better.

"But look for Christ and you will find Him,
and with Him everything else..."

- C. S. Lewis

CHAPTER FOURTEEN

Fixing Your Eyes On Jesus

Therefore, we also,
since we are surrounded,
by so great a cloud of witnesses,
let us lay aside every weight,
and the sin that so greatly ensnares us,
and let us run with endurance the race that is set before us,
looking unto Jesus, the author and finisher of our faith,
who for the joy that was set before Him.
HEBREWS 12:1-2

I got to thinking about the word, "fixing" or "looking." What does that really mean? "The action of deciding or planning something, or fastening something in place." Both of these definitions pertain to our subject. The first directs us to focusing our attention on God. Making a conscious decision to do so. Not wavering but setting our gaze upon Him. The second also refers to fastening ourselves to God. I love that. For us to be so linked with Him that we never let go. This book is all about sanctification and the journey that God has us on in order to mature us in our faith. Strengthening us as we become a more solid believer. What better way to do that than to link ourselves to Him. Forever. When we become a believer, we are linked to God. We are given a promise, and He won't ever let us go. We need to truly focus on Him through the tough times, the ups and downs of life. At times we may step away from praying, or following God, but He is always there pulling us back.

I am so very thankful that He kept a hold of me, no matter what happened in my life. I have watched baptisms of older people who share how they went astray for many years, but returned to Him. Or maybe they were not from a believing home, but a neighbor shared the gospel with them, or took them to church, and then later they remembered what they had learned. Maybe those people were not walking with Jesus, but He did not forget about them.

> *"Therefore as you have received Christ Jesus the Lord, so walk in Him, having been firmly rooted and now being built up in Him and established in your faith, just as you were instructed, and overflowing with gratitude." Colossians 2:6-7*

Walking in Jesus is mentioned many times in scripture and refers to a daily exercise. Constantly focusing on the Lord needs to be the pattern for our life. This behavior will establish our maturity in our faith.

> *"I was very glad to find some of your children walking in truth, just as we have received commandment to do from the Father. Now I ask you, lady, not as though I were writing to you a new commandment, but the one which we have had from the beginning, that we love one another. And this is love, that we walk according to His commandments. This is the commandment, just as you have heard from the beginning, that you should walk in it." 2 John 1:4-6*

John writes this as a measure of obedience. We are to walk as He wants us to walk, as we follow Him and His commandments. I mentioned earlier in this book that one of my favorite books that has been a "go-to" for me is "Fix Your Eyes On Jesus" by Anne Ortlund. It was originally written in 1991, and yet it is so very pertinent for today. It still holds true that we need practical advice on everyday living for Christ. Our vision improves as our faith matures and our spiritual life deepens.

Fixing our eyes on Jesus is hard when we go through difficult times.

> *"For it was fitting for Him, for whom are all things, and through whom are all things, in bringing many sons to glory, to perfect the author of their salvation through sufferings. Both for He who sanctifies and those who are sanctified are all from one Father; for which reason He is not ashamed to call them brethren, saying, "I WILL PROCLAIM YOUR NAME TO MY BRETHREN, IN THE MIDST OF THE CONGREGATION I WILL SING YOUR PRAISE." And again, "I WILL PUT MY TRUST IN HIM." And again, "BEHOLD, I AND THE CHILDREN WHOM GOD HAS GIVEN ME." Hebrews 2:10-13*

There is a young woman in our church who shared her story with me on how she has learned through suffering to continue to look to Jesus.

> *Nearly before giving birth to my first beautiful baby, my husband, who was working nights, came home to wake me up with news that my brother, who is and will always be my little brother, had died in a motorcycle accident. He was in his early 20s. My world had shattered. "God why?!" was all I could say over and over, and honestly still to this day I ask "God why?!" That was almost 14 years ago, but God continues to give me the answer to the question.*

Saying "God why" brought me so many frustrations but also opportunities. He gave me people in my life to talk to who have been through a multitude of issues that I could now understand because of what happened in my life. From a girl who was hooked on heroin to a girl who also lost her brother in a car accident to another girl who doesn't know her own "why" in her life. It's weird to say: I'm grateful that I have these opportunities. It's grown my faith - if my tragedy can help even one person with one conversation to know that God is good, loving and will be with you, then it makes it a little better each time.

Learning to grow in knowing God isn't easy, it's a process. That's what sanctification is all about. He never told us it would be easy, and it's still not. Daily I yearn for the day when I will see my brother again. For now, I will do my best to continue to serve God, and the people who need serving, and tell sweet and funny stories to my girls about their Uncle while God keeps growing me.

Jessica T.

I am thankful that Jessica could share this story with us even though I am sure the wound still feels fresh. Losing a sibling is such a difficult thing, and we always question when young people die.

God works in our lives, and He works through suffering. He sanctifies us, preparing us for service. God is working on our lives as we focus on Him and are obedient. Fixing our eyes on Him. One thing Anne Ortlund shares is this prayer, which is appropriate for all of us as believers.

"Lord, for my own maturing, to make me more like Christ, You've allowed me to participate in His sufferings. I'm awed. I'm honored to be in such company. That's a big deal. But, Lord, I choose to belittle my own feelings. They're not a big deal. Keep me from

retaliation, real or imagined; keep me from filling my thoughts with self-pity and fresh self-woundings and all over-occupation with myself. Lord, keep my heart and life concerned for others. Lord, give me true compassion for my oppressors. And, Lord, I entrust myself totally to You. Into Your good hands I commit my spirit. Amen."[12]

We need to release things to God. It frees us.

When you fix your eyes on Jesus you are not looking at yourself. You are not worrying about everything. He grants you such joy no matter your circumstances. He forgives your sins, redeems you, blesses you.

"Finally brethren, whatever is true, whatever is honorable, whatever is right, whatever is pure, whatever is lovely, whatever is of good repute, if there is any excellence and if anything worthy of praise, dwell on these things. The things you have learned and received and heard and seen in me, practice these things, and the God of peace will be with you." Philippians 4:8-9

Believers are to think of God's standard of holiness. These attributes help us to concentrate on God. He gives us perfect peace. If we are so busy worrying about life it can rob us of our joy, and then our eyes are not fixed on Jesus.

"For this reason I say to you, do not be worried about your life, as to what you will eat or what you will drink; nor for your body, as to what you will put on. Is life not more than food, and the body more than clothing? Look at the birds of the sky, that they do not sow, nor reap, nor gather crops into barns, and yet your heavenly

12 Anne Ortlund, *Fix Your Eyes on Jesus,* (United States: Word Publishing, 1991), 67.

Father feeds them. Are you not much more important than they? And which of you by worrying can add a single day to his life's span? And why are you worried about clothing? Notice how the lilies of the field grow; they do not labor nor do they spin thread for cloth, yet I say to you that not even Solomon in all his glory clothed himself like one of these. But if God so clothes the grass of the field, which is alive today and tomorrow is thrown into the furnace, will He not much more clothe you? You of little faith! Do not worry then, saying, 'What are we to eat?' or 'What are we to drink?' or 'What are we to wear for clothing?' For the Gentiles eagerly seek all these things; for your heavenly Father knows that you need all these things. But seek first His kingdom and His righteousness, and all these things will be provided to you. "So do not worry about tomorrow; for tomorrow will worry about itself. Each day has enough trouble of its own." Matthew 6:25-34

This passage is such a comfort to me. We have full provision from God. We do not need to worry. Worry takes our eyes off God. I look back on my life, and all the hard things about growing up. I know I was concerned, but I saw God provide for us. My birthday is at Thanksgiving time. When Lisa, my sister, was in college, she mailed me a t-shirt from her school. I received it the Friday after Thanksgiving. It was my only gift that year, but I was SO stoked. I received a present! Perspective. Sometimes kids asked me what I got for Christmas when I got back to school in January. I remember lying. I made up things. All I had gotten was socks and a slip. Until someone asked, I wasn't concerned about not having much. I think what we may think of as someone else's expectations can also take our eyes off of Him and give us cause to worry. It did for me.

We now live in an AI world. It is difficult sometimes to know what is real and what is not real. But we have God's Word and the more we study it, the more we see who God is and that He is very real.

But we need to fix our eyes on Him. Things distract us from that goal. My mind flits to a hundred different things…ALL THE TIME. I know I must keep my focus. I make lists, I keep journals, and pray. God grants me peace and the ability to look to Him. My melancholy personality can be a blessing and a curse. I examine everything in my head. It is amazing how in the past several years, after decades of being concerned that someone did not like me, it does not matter that much anymore. I began to realize that it wasn't always about me, sometimes it was about them. Worrying about what others thought about me took my eyes off God and onto me.

Keep fervent in prayer. Share your needs and concerns, keep communication with God. Do not let go of the truth that He loves you. FIX YOUR EYES ON HIM.

"When grace begins to rule, then our preoccupation with ourselves begins to leave."

- Alistair Begg

CHAPTER FIFTEEN

Dedicate Your Life

Let your heart therefore be wholly devoted
to the Lord our God,
to walk in His statutes
and to keep His commandments,
as at this day."
I Kings 8:61

So my friend, as we have been looking at many testimonies from those who love God but have still gone through great hardship, we see in His Word that He shapes us through various trials and struggles. We can see that He has a plan for us, and we can grow to love Him more than ever. That doesn't mean that God will never throw us a curveball. Matter of fact, He will still continue to mold us like clay. The following testimony of this young woman shows us that the unexpected can and will happen.

I always knew that following Jesus wouldn't mean an easy life. I understood early on that the Christian walk would include trials, valleys, and moments of pain. But even with that knowledge, nothing could have prepared me for the 3 seconds that changed my life forever.

It happened in the middle of something so normal—something I had done countless times before. It was November of 2012 and I was a 15-year-old, Level 9 competitive gymnast, practicing a skill I had completed hundreds of times. One wrong move, one split-second miscalculation, and I was on the mat—unable to move. In an instant, I went from being a strong, athletic young woman to being completely paralyzed from the chest down.

The diagnosis was a spinal cord injury. Permanent. Life-altering. That moment marked the beginning of a new chapter, not just physically, but spiritually. Suddenly, everything I once relied on—my strength, my independence, my dreams—was gone. All I had left was my faith. And I quickly discovered that my faith in Jesus would have to be my everything.

This wasn't the beginning of my relationship with Christ. I had already been saved for years. I had already declared Him Lord of my life. But this was a season where now I had to live like I believed it. This was the path after grace—where salvation met suffering, and faith had to become action.

There were dark days. I cried out to God. I wrestled with grief, with disappointment, even with anger. But He never left me. In fact, He met me in those lowest places with a peace I couldn't explain. Over and over again, I heard His voice in the quiet: "My grace is sufficient for you, for My power is made perfect in weakness" 2 Corinthians 12:9 (NIV).

Through this new reality of mine, God began to strip away the things I thought defined me and reminded me of who I truly was: His daughter. Chosen. Loved. Held. My identity was no longer in my abilities or accomplishments—it was in Christ alone.

The Lord helped me decide to turn my pain into purpose. I started to share my story—not because it was easy to talk about, but because I knew others needed to see what it looks like when God carries someone through the fire and refines them into something even more beautiful.

If just one person finds Christ because of my testimony, it has all been worth it. If my journey can help someone else see Jesus more clearly, then I'll keep telling it. Even in my paralysis, God has opened doors I never expected. I may not walk physically, but I walk in faith every single day. And the Lord has never failed me.

Romans 8:28 has anchored me throughout this journey: "And we know that in all things God works for the good of those who love Him, who have been called according to His purpose."(NIV). I believe that. Not because life has gone how I planned, but because even when it didn't, God was still good.

This is what the path after grace looks like—it's not without hardship, but it's full of God's presence. It's where faith is tested, refined, and made real. It's where we learn that grace doesn't just save us—it sustains us. And it's where we begin to realize that even our greatest suffering can become a stage for God's glory.

I may perhaps never walk again in this life, but I know I will dance in eternity. And until then, I'll keep moving forward—carried by His grace, strengthened by His Word, and led by His love.

Jacoby

I do not personally know this young woman, but I have to say, she has a better perspective on God's purposes than many much older than herself. Her life may seem like a tragedy to some, but she has dedicated it to God, and He is using her for His glory. God sustains us through whatever journey He puts us on.

Her story challenges us all to think about how we would react during an inconceivable adversity. Would we lean in to God? As I wrap up this book, what more is there to say? Jacoby perfectly describes the path after grace. If just one person is helped by hearing her story it is worth it. I have also thought this as I write books. I am not a famous author, and do not sell tons of books, but then someone shares how one of my books has helped them. God wants us to share what He has done in our lives in order to encourage others and to remind us of His love for us.

"Come and hear, all who fear God, And I will tell of what He has done for my soul." Psalm 66:16

"Then the LORD answered me and said, "Record the vision And inscribe it on tablets, That the one who reads it may run." Habakkuk 2:2

We need to document how God has worked in our lives so that 100 years from now, people will see. God commands us over and over.

"Return to your house and describe what great things God has done for you." So he went away, proclaiming throughout the whole city what great things Jesus had done for him." Luke 8:39

And the testimony of Jesus' blood is the ultimate testimony for believers.

"And they overcame him because of the blood of the Lamb and because of the word of their testimony, and they did not love their life even when faced with death." Revelation 12:11

Testimonies transform lives, and I hope you always share yours with those around you. God takes us on this long journey, molding and pruning us, and directs us in the way we should go. How can we serve? What is our purpose?

I had so many "bright ideas" (ha) on what it looked like to serve God. It turned out that He had a different plan than I originally thought. Now at 66, I feel like I am rushing to do what He originally intended for me. We need to fully trust His glorious plan for each of us and embrace it. God desires our intimacy with Him. Jacoby reminds us that He sustains us. Continue to move forward beloved. We are still on the journey.

"I still believe that standing up for the truth of God is the greatest thing in the world. This is the end of life. The end of life is not to be happy. The end of life is not to achieve pleasure and avoid pain. The end of life is to do the will of God, come what may."

- Rev. Dr. Martin Luther King, Jr.

CHAPTER 16

Conclusion

"For whether we live, we live unto the Lord;
and whether we die, we die unto the Lord:
whether we live therefore,
or die, we are the Lords."
ROMANS 14:8

I have mentioned my moma throughout this book. The way God changed her attitude and life was an example to everyone around her . Those who didn't know her during her previous years were now recipients of her caring temperament. Some, like myself, had difficulty trusting the change. But after seeing how God used a life of terrible situations for her to become more like Him, I know she was transformed miraculously. From her father dying when she was 5, to raising her brother while her mom worked, to losing 10 babies and adopting Lisa and I, and then losing her husband. She was transformed.

We do not know what tomorrow may bring. Had you asked me ten years ago if I would have 7 books published, I would have thought you crazy. I would have said, "I am not a writer." But God told me someone needed to tell my story, and share God's Word with others. I can use His Word, and testimonies of those that love Him, to give hope to others. I began this ministry when I was in my fifties. I hope to continue to serve Him, in whatever way He has for me, until He calls me home. I am the Lord's. He may teach us a lesson that we were not prepared for, and it may be difficult to bear. But this I know, He has a greater purpose beyond what I understand.

The great women's Bible teacher, Kay Arthur, went home to glory recently. She was dear to my heart. I have been a Precepts teacher for almost a decade. Precepts is a ministry Kay began many years ago. It focuses on learning God's Word, and has in-depth Bible study materials. It teaches you to look at every chapter closely, and ask what it is saying, and why it is there. It has you underline places, people, and phrases. I have done this for so long now, that even on Sunday mornings, as I am listening to our pastor, I look at the passage and look at the big picture and what it means. The comments all over social media after Kay's death, had a common theme. Her greatest desire was to teach God's Word, and for others to learn how to study it. She loved God's Word. My greatest prayer is to follow that example:to continue to study, and really know God, and be able to teach others to do that as well.

So although God may still give us hard times, and may still take us on a path we do not understand, I want to stay the course and not let the things of this life push me off the path - the path to spiritual maturity.

I am now 66 years old. I have always been young at heart and felt young. My husband, Craig, is 5 years younger. And maybe my outdoorsy, beach bum attitude keeps me young. But in the past few years, I admit to thinking that I may not have more than 15 or 20 years left to encourage loved ones in their faith. I feel a sense of urgency. I have always wanted my kids and grandkids to know and love God, but now I feel so intensely about it, that every time I am in the tub or shower I start crying as I pray to God for them to love Him and live for Him. I love this quote by Elisabeth Elliot: *"It is God to whom and with whom we travel, and while He is the end of our journey, He is also at every stopping place."*

SO, as my journey is getting closer to the end, I am praying more. And I commit to praying at least three times every day for my kids, their spouses, their kids, my husband, my cousins, my siblings. I will always desire for them to know God, serve Him and share their faith with others until my path runs out.

> *"We must work the works of Him who sent me as long as it is day; night is coming, when no one can work." John 9:4*

> *"Therefore be on the alert, for you do not know which day your Lord is coming. But be sure of this, that if the head of the house had known at what time of the night the thief was coming, he would have been on the alert and would not have allowed his house to be broken into. For this reason you also must be ready; for the Son of Man is coming at an hour when you do not think He will." Matthew 24:42-44*

Beloved, where are you in your journey? Do you know the Lord? Does He direct your steps on your path? Churches don't preach fire and brimstone much anymore but eternity is a long time. Where will you spend it? With God or separated from Him? I pray for those who read my books. I am praying for you. For your eternity. And for your maturing in your walk with the Lord.

A Disciples Renewal

O my Savior, help me.
I am so slow to learn, so prone to forget, so weak to climb;
I am in the foothills when I should be on the heights;
I am pained by my graceless heart,
my prayerless days,
my poverty of love,
my sloth in the heavenly race,
my sullied conscience,
my wasted hours,
my unspent opportunities.
I am blind while light shines around me;
take the scales from my eyes,
grind to dust the evil heart of unbelief.
Make it my chiefest joy to study thee,
meditate on thee,
gaze on thee,
sit like Mary at thy feet,
lean like John on thy breast,
appeal like Peter to thy love,
count like Paul all things dung.
Give me increase and progress in grace
so that there may be
more decision in my character,
more vigour in my purposes,
more elevation in my life,
more fervour in my devotion,
more constancy in my zeal.
As I have a position in the world,
keep me from making the world my position;
May I never seek in the creature

what can be found only in the Creator;
Let not faith cease from seeking thee
until it vanishes into sight.
Ride forth in me, thou King of kings and Lord of lords,
that I may live victoriously, and in victory attain my end.

- Old Puritan Prayer[13]

13 Arthur Bennett, *The Valley of Vision: A Collection of Puritan Prayers and Devotions* (United Kingdom: Banner of Truth Trust).

Photo by Sarah White

Thank you for reading *The Path After Grace: A Journey.* I hope I have encouraged you in your walk of faith. For more information on all my books, visit my website at **www.liveboldlyministries.com**. From the website you can also access my video series and podcasts.

I would really appreciate a brief review of this book on your favorite review sites or the website where you purchased this book. Thank you.

BIBLIOGRAPHY

Mrs. Charles E. Cowman, *Streams in the Desert,* (Grand Rapids, MI: Zondervan Publishing House, 1996), 114-115.

Dane Ortlund, *Gentle and Lowly,* (Wheaton, IL: Crossway, 2020), 13.

J.I. Packer, *A Quest for Godliness* (Wheaton, IL: Crossway Books, 1990), 116.

Jerry Bridges, *The Pursuit of Holiness,* (Colorado Springs,CO: NavPress, 2006), xi-xii.

Jerry Bridges, *The Discipline of Grace* (Colorado Springs, CO: NavPress, 2006), 2.

Karen Foster, *Lunches with Loretta* (United States: Karen Foster, 2020), 5, 11 and 13.

John MacArthur, *The Keys to Spiritual Growth,* (Old Tappan, NJ: Fleming H. Revell Company, 1976), 47-48.

Howard G. Hendricks and William D. Hendricks, *Living by the Book* (Chicago, IL: Moody, 1991), 292.

Anne Ortlund, *Fix Your Eyes on Jesus* (United States: Word Publishing, 1991), 67.

Arthur Bennett, *The Valley of Vision: A Collection of Puritan Prayers and Devotions* (United Kingdom: Banner of Truth Trust).

CONTRIBUTORS

Testimonies Provided by:

Melanie Keyes
Spencer Boliou
Karen Herd
Roger Saunders
Michael Keyes
Jim Herd
John Bryant
Andrea Taddicken
Cliff Loeffler
Mark McCutchan
Jessica Taddicken
Jacoby Miles

Epigraphs provided by:

David Platt
Martin Luther
Roger Saunders
Amy Carmichael
John Piper
Jessica Faith Hagen
C.S. Lewis
Jerry Bridges
Jim Elliot
Francis Chan
Jeremiah Burroughs
Charles Spurgeon
Elisabeth Elliot
Alistair Begg
Rev. Dr. Martin Luther King, Jr.

liveboldlyministries.com

NICKI'S BOOKS

LIVE BOLDLY MINISTRIES

When I started writing books, I wasn't sure how far it would go. I just wanted to share Christ with as many people as possible, and offer help, and encouragement. Now, with seven published books, Live Boldly Ministries has grown to far more than I ever thought, and I am blessed to be surrounded by a wonderful team with a vision for spreading God's Word and His love to those around us.

Meet the Team:

Nicki White - Founder/Author/Speaker
Jessica Everett - Executive Administrator/Marketing
Re Loeffler - Editor/Advisor/Assistant Administrator
Craig White - Tech Advisor
Lisa Shumaker - Advisor/Outreach
Jamie Hudson - Photographer
Rafael Amaro - Website
Marsha Philbrook - Editor
Karen Law - Libraries
Linda Saracoff - Social Media/Prayer Team
Jim and Karen Herd - Social Media/Prayer Team
Priscilla Robinson - Prayer Team
Nancy Jindrich - Prayer Team
Cindy Saracoff - Prayer Team
Jeanette Dickey - Prayer Team
Amy Crist - Prayer Team

ACKNOWLEDGEMENTS

Craig White ~ I am so thankful for a husband who supports this ministry. He is encouraging, and helps with tech support and ideas, and has supported these endeavors financially, never complaining.

Jessica Everett ~ She has met with me every week, sometimes many times, for 8 years now. She takes care of endless emails, and helps with tech and ideas.

Re Loeffler ~ She has stayed up late editing to meet a deadline. She is so detail oriented that she can find the smallest detail I would miss. So thankful for all her many hours of work.

Lisa Shumaker ~ my amazing sister. She has been so encouraging and supportive, along with her husband, Sam. I admit to some tears being shed at times when we have talked about our moma.

Carpenter's Son Publishing, Shane Crabtree ~ They have always been encouraging to me, even when I sell so few books for them. And I probably call with silly questions, but they never make me feel like they don't want me to contact them.

Tammy Kling ~ my content editor. She is always inspirational, and makes me feel like I can do anything. She always tells me she loves each book. I get off the phone with her and am greatly encouraged.

Joni Baker ~ Buoyancy PR, my publicist who gets me radio and tv interviews. I appreciate her legwork for each project.

Jamie Hudson ~ I am so thankful she has taken so many photos through the years. I do not like photos of myself, but she has made me look so professional.

Team 3:12 as we call it, based on Colossians 3:12 ~ each person adds something to our team, and I could not do any of this without them.

Rosemary Gifford ~ beta-reader. Thank you for your help and suggestions.

CONTACT US

Nicki Corinne White is available for book signings and speaking engagements. To get in touch with her team, please email us or message us through her website.

nickicorinnewhite@gmail.com
www.liveboldlyministries.com

ABOUT THE AUTHOR

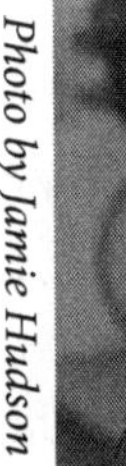

Photo by Jamie Hudson

NICKI CORINNE WHITE has a passion for studying and teaching God's Word. She has been leading Bible studies and discipling young women for many years. She is very involved in her local church with both the children's ministry and women's ministry. She has a tender heart for those who are hurting and those who are new to church. Nicki hopes to be an encouragement to those around her by lending a listening ear, kind word, or a biblical reminder. She also opens her home to share with others, serves others through hospitality on a regular basis, and believes we are all called to do this.

Nicki was also a finalist for the American Legacy Book Awards in 2024. She feels blessed to have been able to use her story and personal experience to encourage others, and hopes to expand this ministry through her writing and speaking.

Nicki is married to her husband, Craig. She has four children and currently has 9 grandchildren.